The Kindness of Strangers

University of Iowa Press, Iowa City

THE KIND NESS OF STRAN GERS

TOM LUTZ

University of Iowa Press, Iowa City 52242
Copyright © 2021 by the University of Iowa Press
www.uipress.uiowa.edu
Printed in the United States of America

Design by Kristina Kachele Design, llc

Printed on acid-free paper

Library of Congress Cataloging-in-Publication Data
Names: Lutz, Tom, author.
Title: The Kindness of Strangers / by Tom Lutz.
Description: Iowa City: University of Iowa Press, 2021. |
Includes index.
Identifiers: LCCN 2021004315 (print) |
LCCN 2021004316 (ebook) | ISBN
9781609387884 (paperback) | ISBN 9781609387891 (ebook)
Subjects: LCSH: Lutz, Tom—Travel. | Travel—Social aspects. |
Kindness. | Voyages and travels. | Travelers' writings, American.
Classification: LCC G226.L87 A3 2021 (print) |
LCC G226.L87 (ebook) | DDC
910.4092—dc23
LC record available at https://lccn.loc.gov/2021004315
LC ebook record available at https://lccn.loc.gov/2021004316

To Jesse and Guillermo, Yarrow and Ken, Cody and April
—fellow travelers

CONTENTS

AT HOME IN THE WORLD

Travel leaves you speechless, and turns you into a storyteller.

. . .

Travel gives you a home in a thousand strange places,
and leaves you a stranger in your own land.
—*Ibn Battuta*, A Gift to Those Who Contemplate the
Wonders of Cities and the Marvels of Traveling *(ca. 1360)*

In Monday, a note was slipped under my door saying the hotel would be shutting down on Thursday. My flight to the highlands of Papua New Guinea, which had been postponed, was set now to leave Manila on Wednesday, so this news didn't add to my distress. There were reports of tribal violence, which erupts sporadically, and because of spotty internet, I was having trouble getting in touch with a hotel there. Although it was not unusual for me, I knew very little about what to expect when I landed, and although I discounted the reports of violence on the alarmist state department pages, lurking in the background was the worry about this new virus. In early March 2020, we knew a bit about what we would shortly learn to call COVID-19, but not much. The first person-to-person transmission in the US had been confirmed just a month earlier, on January 30, and the Chinese news services were quoting doctors saying that the virus would peak in ten days. The first person to die from the virus outside China did so in the Philippines on February 2, but he was a man from Wuhan. The first death in the US happened just a week before I got on my plane, and a number of European countries were announcing their first cases of infection. Travel warnings were sounded for early hotspots—South Korea, Iran, and Italy—and the WHO had declared it a global emergency, but I, stupid American, thought: *What are the chances? There isn't a single case in Papua New Guinea, and I probably have more chance getting caught in the tribal violence than getting the disease.* Then there was malaria, dengue, and rest of the tropical dangers awaiting. Why worry about this disease that has only killed one person?

That Tuesday, deaths in the US hit yet another new record—seven. The Philippine president told people that the disease was spreading and that if they wanted to go home to their families in the countryside, they should do it now, as he would be locking down the capital. A new note came through saying the hotel would close Wednesday. Belatedly, it dawned on me: the danger wasn't that I would get the disease, the danger was that I would be patient zero in New Guinea. My safety wasn't the issue, my vector was. A new note slipped under the door. The hotel would close the next day. I called the airlines, canceled my New Guinea flight and booked one home, arranged a taxi with the front desk. A new note slid under the door. The hotel would close in twelve hours.

Wednesday morning, I went to the lobby to check out and head to the airport. The president had shut down the taxis. The lobby was mobbed as people scrambled to find a way to leave. Four of us agreed to pay a freelancer to take us to the airport in his van.

Home again, I saw that the panic had quadrupled in the few short days I was gone. The US death toll had been steadily rising, and on March 15, fifteen people died, twenty-two on the sixteenth, and odd as it seems now, with over three thousand people dying a day, those numbers were frightening. By the end of March, the US would have its first day with a thousand deaths, and the new normal was underway. The new normal meant, for most of us, sheltering at home. Indefinitely.

And so I write this introduction from a world in which travel—nonessential travel, as it is called—has been abolished. Vaccines have been approved, and that gives us hope; we wonder whether they will work, how long they will work, whether the virus's mutations will prove them ineffective, whether each inoculation will last a year or a month. Will there be enough for those of us who are nonessential? I won't lie, it gives a bittersweet tinge to the editing process for this book—is this the end of the road, at least for me? Will I get to write volume four? Or is this the last hurrah?

This is the third book in a series that I had been calling, just to myself until now, *At Home in the World*. I had compiled the first two volumes, *Drinking Mare's Milk on the Roof of the World* and *And the Monkey Learned Nothing*, and part of this one into a massive collage, encompassing some thousand pages, divided into twenty sections, with each of those fifty-page sections composed of nine anecdotal sketches arranged from short to longer to short again—arbitrarily, that is, each section was shaped like a fifty-page standard distribution curve, repeated twenty times. I decided that at least four continents had to be represented in each of the twenty sections, and that no countries could be represented more than once in any one section.

To put this crazy hodgepodge together required color-coding all the pieces I had written and cutting and pasting them into various possible arrangements, trying to maintain a feeling of both randomness and design, an accidental, intentional patchwork that had a haphazard yet coherent aesthetic. It was a big, stark-raving mad, beautiful, volume—or so I thought—and my fondest hope for it was that it might end up in people's bathrooms, a book no one would ever read cover to cover, any more than one would read an encyclopedia that way. Readers would just dip into it haphazardly, tasting a tiny piece or a small piece or a longer piece, maybe even two, and then calling it a day. I didn't want people to read it so much as read *in* it, as one would do with a miscellany, an anthology.

The organization of that fat volume was informed by Oulipo (short for *Ouvroir de littérature potentielle*, or the Workshop for Potential Literature) the Parisian (at first) literary movement that believes that artificial constraints are generative, that they are the essence of art. Think of the sonnet as a form or pointillism as a technique, where you have to follow a strict rule or rules, and those rules make the piece precisely what it becomes. Some Oulipian pieces have become famous, like Georges Perec's *La Disparition*, which was written without using the most common letter in the French language, *e*, or Walter Abish's *Alphabetical Africa*, which gives itself a series of alphabetical constraints (the first chapter only uses words that start with *a*, the second chapter words that start with *a* or *b*, etc.). The constraints I gave myself included the ones I've mentioned and three more: (1) they would all stick to something like the classical unities—Aristotle said the best work had unity of time (happening all in a single day), unity of place (all happening in the same geographical space), and unity of action (representing a single principal action); (2) each piece would begin in media res and end in media res; and (3) I wouldn't name any hotels or restaurants or landmarks, trying to veer as strongly away from travel journalism as possible, allowing the stories to remain slightly untethered, and thereby feel less like the stuff of guidebooks and more like the stuff of fiction. Whether or not I was successful at that, I wrote the pieces, laid them all out, moved them around until each section felt right, then moved the sections around until that arrangement felt right, and constructed my wild book.

But for some reason, nobody wanted to publish a thousand-page book of strange travel anecdotes, arranged in a bizarre, arbitrary way, with no narrative arc, no connective tissue, and no apparent reason for being, written by a writer with no track record or established audience in travel writing. None of the twenty publishers who looked at it wanted it. Go figure! O, where are the audacious, risk-taking publishers of yesteryear?

And so I took the monster apart and made some reasonably sized books out of it, giving them each a more conventional organization—chronological in the first volume, by continent in the second. The first book had anecdotes from many different times in my life, with some of the original pieces stitched together, making the pieces longer and more narrative. The second has pieces from the last decade or so. And in this volume, everything is from the last four or five years.

Gertrude Stein, in explaining how she amassed such an amazing art collection, said a person had to choose: one could either buy clothes or buy art, and she had always chosen the latter. I'd like to amend that to say one can either buy clothes or buy art or buy travel, and I've always chosen the third. I dress like Gertrude Stein— more or less frumpy and far from stylish—and I own no art, save some books and a few pieces my daughter and a friend made and gave me.

I've long since given up explaining why, in this life of mine, an eternal restlessness keeps me on the move. Bruce Chatwin tells us restlessness is the norm, that civilization, by which he means sedentary bourgeoise life, is bad for our health, bad for our emotional life, and bad for our species. We are meant to move, disquiet is a fundamental trait of our species, and we resist it or let it go dormant at our peril. I of course like this argument—it makes me out as a healthy nomad, not a crackpot running around on the universe's largest hamster wheel. But either way, like Chatwin, run I must. And I feel compelled to keep writing about it too. "O public road," as Whitman, one of the great wanderers, wrote, "You express me better than I can express myself, / You shall be more to me than my poem." Yes, perhaps. But as Whitman's massive poem suggests, travel and its expression are not either/or. As Ibn Battuta puts it, a journey can both leave you speechless and turn you into a storyteller.

There exists in our current literary culture an argument—the key word in the argument is "appropriation"—that suggests that for me to represent people in a culture not my own is ethically suspect; that only locals should write about their locality, only Samoans should write about Samoans; that anything else is colonialist appropriation of the experience of others. I believe this is stupendously misguided. I believe women, for instance, should not only be able to write about men, but that the world would be a poorer place, and literature would be near useless, if they did not. And the logic of appropriation also suggests that reading about people different from oneself—since reading is a coproduction of writer and reader—is also ethically suspect. If I believed that representing the world around us in as much of its complexity as possible was wrong or had no value, or that reading about the world around us as broadly and inclusively as possible was wrong and had no value, I would stop writing and burn all my books. And stop reading. Instead, I offer these little forays into the world, these stories of my encounters with people with very different backgrounds and current situations from my own, in the belief that the exact opposite is true—that the most important job literary writing can do is bring us reports about our encounters with others, reports from elsewhere.

This is my report for now.

Like most people, I have no idea when I'll be on the road again. Until then, words will have to do.

PHILIPPINES

His left hand was mangled. A huge gash ran up the young man's palm from between his thumb and forefinger toward his wrist, and the two smaller fingers were curled into a crusty red-brown-black ball—maybe a joint or two were missing? A massive aging scab covered it all. The scab had cracked open and recoagulated many times, or so it seemed, with different layers of red, maroon, brown, and black. It was hard to look at. Whatever happened had happened a while ago, maybe a month or more back. He was in his mid or at most late twenties, waiting to nab a tourist at the top of the path that runs down to the Batad rice terraces. This was a few years before the world shut down for the coronavirus.

"What happened to your hand?" I asked.

"Accident," he said. "Making house."

"Did you go to a doctor?"

"Yes, midwife."

"Is there no doctor here?"

"Yes, midwife. I am good guide."

We were in northern Luzon, the middle of nowhere, near Banaue, miles from a town of any size, in small but rugged mountains. The sun was hot and high, undiminished by a stuttering, tepid breeze.

"Can't I just walk to Batad by myself?"

"No."

"It's right down this path, isn't it?"

"Yes, but—"

He was quiet. Not pushy. Reserved. He was a good-looking kid, with a boy-band sweep of dark hair, and boy band–sized too, maybe five-two. A few small scars on his face.

Pictures of Batad, a tiny village set in vast terraced rice fields, are in every guidebook to the Philippines, often making the cover. They swoop up from the valley floor, limning the bowlside of the mountains in fractal rows, elegant, majestic. It's a long ride from Manila to the trail-head, along twisting, shattered mountain roads. I found the spot after passing it a couple of times. More like a driveway than a road, it runs down the hillside only a city block or so before petering out. Weeds grow through cracked concrete, as if the turnoff had tried to become a road but stalled and was now, around the first curve, just a narrow, pockmarked parking lot for the jeeps and jitneys that served the local villagers and, on better days, brought in tourists. It was very quiet. The grass growing around the tires of a couple of the buses said that they hadn't moved in a month or more.

"So you were born here?"

"Yes, in Batad, I show you."

"Maybe," I said. It being off-season, there were many more guides than tourists, and their informal rotation system gave this guy the first shot at me, but I had burnt myself before accepting the first offer.

"And you lived here your whole life?"

"No, one year I work gold mine. Very hard. No gold, so I come back."

"Where was the gold mine?"

"Baguio," he said, pointing over the hill. It was about a hundred miles to the west.

His English wasn't great but not bad, and he was sweet, relaxed. We agreed on a price that was roughly three-quarters his first ask, and I assumed double the norm. He was patient. He knew I was going to say yes before I did.

We started walking to the trail, past the fabulous, garish-painted jitneys. I stopped to take a picture of one with FRANZEN painted across the top, and emailed copies to Don Franzen and Jonathan Franzen. The emails failed. No service.

"What was Baguio like?" I asked. "A bigger town than this, yes?"

He pointed to the north. He shrugged about its size, saying he just worked, nothing more. He had been there for nine months or so, and he had been to Banaue, a little more than nine miles away. He'd never been to Sagada, the other main tourist stop in northern Luzon, about forty miles as the crow flies, but three times that on the mountain roads. He laughed when I asked if he had been to Manila, an eight-hour bus trip south—few people, the laugh suggested, could be expected to have been that far.

Stepping down the precipitous path, we passed a number of people climbing up, some carrying rice sacks and boxes on their heads or shoulders, some women with a kid or two, maybe going to town. Did they do that once a week? Once a month? My guide shrugged when I asked. A couple of men passed us going down too, but moving faster, heavily loaded, bringing in supplies. The path was steep, worn away by rains and reconfigured countless times over the decades, the dirt loose, slippery when there was any gravel—a tough hike, even down-hill. And this unrelenting footpath was the only way in and out of the valley. The guys with seventy-kilo loads, moving fast, had calves the size of shovel blades.

A sweaty hour later we came around the corner and the cover shot was right there: not as green as in the pictures, but the waves of terraces curved softly along the ridge, stretching above and below, a small clump of houses here and there, a village at the bottom of the valley, some of the terraces fallow, some with rice just planted, light green spears in groups of four and eight sticking a few inches out of the brown opaque water.

The terraces are made with a series of earthen retaining walls, maybe narrower than a cinder block, and the only paths through the fields were the tops of those walls. As I started across one, I panicked—I imagined losing my balance, flailing camera-first into the mud—and I realized that my guide, waiting for me to catch up, must have seen hundreds of us tourists mincing forward like me with comic wariness. Why would a person all of a sudden fail to walk in a straight line? Just because there was a four-foot drop to the right was no reason to plunge rightward, but like the people who feel a per-verse urge to throw themselves off a bridge or tall build-ing, I felt the pull of the imagined disaster. If a person came from the other direction, often with a bale of plant material on their heads or cargo hung from the ends of a pole slung across their shoulders, we stepped aside, onto another retaining wall, to let them pass. Whoever had the heavier load had the right of way, and that always meant locals.

We stopped at a small kiosk that sold candy, cigarettes, and sundries, and had a shaded platform with plastic footstools for seating. It stood on stilts over the terraces as they fell away below. The owner, a twenty-year-old guy with a countercultural goatee and a few amateur tats, sat, calm, his toddler son at his feet. The kid started to play hide-and-seek with me, leaning around the edge of the counter, which meant he was dangling twenty feet or more in the air. I was snapping his picture, and he'd crane over to see. The father had grown up, I realized, in this same hybrid of earth and sky, and remained as unconcerned as his son about the two-story drop.

A couple of girls came in and bought a pack of gum. I asked for bottles of water for me and my guide. I paid and said keep the change.

"Why?" the shopkeeper asked, with an edge—*I don't need your fucking charity*, it implied.

"As a gift for your son," I said, "for letting me take his picture."

He shrugged, as if to say maybe that was fair, and kept the change, although he didn't seem much happier about it. A little, maybe. Maybe it was a legitimate exchange, not insulting foreign aid.

My guide didn't want to accept the water I bought for him either.

"I'll carry it for you," he said.

"It's just a tip," I said. "In advance."

That made it okay, and he snapped it open.

"Are you married?" I asked.

"Yes," he said. "Three children. Only one wife."

"You want only one wife?" I asked. He shrugged, more yes than no.

"You are in love?"

"Of course!" he smiled. "She is very beautiful, very good. I will show you my house."

"Salamat," I said. He looked at me funny, so I asked: "That means *thank you*, right?"

"Salamat is Tagalog," he said.

"How do you say *thank you* in Ifugao?"

"Tank you," he said.

"In Ifugao?"

"Yes, tank you."

We walked across the rest of the fields, then up the hill, crossing back toward the path we had come down. At the edge of the field, a boy ran up and hugged his leg for a split second and ran off.

"This is my house," he said, pointing. It was about twenty feet by twenty feet, held up by eight-foot poles on the downhill side and hovering just a foot off the ground toward the hill. Some of the construction was with unhewn poles, six inches in diameter for posts, three or four inches for the rafters—small trees or tops of bigger ones. The cross beams were rough-sawn lumber, from a local mill, but still, I realized, all of it had to be hauled down the steep hill from the road, as did the cement for the pads the poles sat on. Someone had carried the tin roof panels and the tin sides on their backs down the hill, and the saplings that held up a tin porch roof. He could have mangled his hand on just about any part of it.

It was solid if amateur work, small, and far from finished. He was very proud of it.

His wife came out. I had expected, from the way he talked about her, to see a very beautiful young woman, but that is not the first thing most people would say about her. She was solid, grounded, perhaps more aware of what makes the world go around than her husband, perhaps more practical and more mature and certainly less forthcoming. She was sturdy, nicely unflappable, and not acutely interested in the latest tourist her husband happened to be showing around. She met my eye, was polite, and then disappeared. He watched her as she went. He was in love. The boy who hugged his leg was his middle son. The oldest was eleven.

"Will you vote in the coming election?" I asked him after his wife left. It was a month away and a major topic of conversation in the capital.

"Yes!" he said with a slightly raised eyebrow—an eyebrow that was a kind of challenge: *who would ask something like that?*

"For who?"

"This I shouldn't say!" he said, and he wasn't kidding— he considered it private information, which made sense in a country with partisan violence. We talked about various politicians. Marcos he had liked. Ninoy, no.

"And Obama?" I asked, still the US president at that point, at the very end of his second term.

No recognition.

"Barack Obama? Our president in America, President Barack Obama?"

He screwed up his face, thinking.

"I think I saw on TV once," he said. "But no. Maybe."

He started to walk me up the hill.

"You don't need to walk me back up," I said, handing him his pay and a good tip. "Unless you want to go up and try to get another tourist."

"Yes?" he asked. "It is too late for more tourists, but I don't mind to go back up, it's in price."

"No, don't bother," I said. "Plenty of people are still walking up, I'll follow them if it isn't clear."

"Okay, good," he said, turning downhill. "Tank you."

He walked away, back toward the beautiful house he was building, with his beautiful wife, and his three beautiful children.

"Digong," a late middle-aged man in a bar and restaurant in downtown Manila said. Rodrigo Duterte, also known as Digong, had been president of the Philippines for just under a year. "He was poor man, fought against Marcos. Now he is multimillionaire."

He said this with a shrug, like *how can the universe be so capricious? How can things go so wrong?*

We were sitting next to each other, the man and I, each at our own tiny round table on the front porch of the restaurant, facing the street. I had stopped there randomly on my walkabout. He was around sixty, straight-backed, trim, with cropped, tight, salt-and-pepper curls on his head, and dark skin, wearing a white barong with gold embroidered trim. It was freshly pressed but not new.

He was proud of having been born on the Fourth of July, in Okinawa. His father was in the US Army, and he had lived in Houston for a while. He had dual citizenship. He liked America. He didn't like Duterte.

"Two percent of politicians are clean," he said. "Ninety-eight percent, dirty. So everything the government do, thirty go to the road, seventy to pocket. Thirty go to school, seventy to pocket."

He analyzed the world through percentages, which, it occurred to me, I did too.

"Eighty-five percent Filipinos like America," he said. "Fifteen percent no."

He said something about 340 hectares that Duterte had ended up owning, about buildings here and there he had gobbled up. But most egregious was that now his daughter was a senator, his wife was a mayor, his son held some office, I didn't catch which. This all started early in his career. They all got in the business.

"Now he is president," the man said, "maybe his dog is elected to Congress."

Like many Filipinos I talked with, the man missed Ferdinand Marcos. He thought Marcos was a great man and wished he was still with us. I said I was confused since I thought Marcos was corrupt too and just as brutal.

"Yes, he was dictator," he said. "But he had direction."

Politics in the Philippines, just like in the US, is about personality and morality as well as more practical issues like economics.

"No, I think Duterte is very good," a cab driver said.

"Why?"

"He don't fuck around," he said. "People do a bad thing, sell drugs, he kill them. He get things done."

"Why can't he stop the Muslim rebels, then?" I asked. "They are a very small number—why doesn't the government just wipe them out?"

"They sell them guns," he said. "The rebels are customers. You don't kill goose."

"The government sells them guns?"

"Who else?" he said.

Walking on a small side street in a random neighborhood, a couple of hours into my day's wander, a man was washing his car in a driveway. He stopped and turned off the hose when I got close. He asked if I was American. I said yes, from Los Angeles.

"Me too!" he said. "I'm from Sacramento. Yes, twenty-three years, loved it. I worked at the best restaurant in Sacramento—the governor, state legislature, basketball players, everyone ate there—best fine-dining restaurant in town, twenty-three years. Now, I'm retired."

"And so you moved here?"

"I'm from here! But, no, I don't know if I can live here all the time. Now, I'm on vacation, this house is my relative's. I'm staying maybe six months. Maybe longer, who knows."

"The city—is it the same as when you were growing up?"

"I grew up poor, and so look at this house—"

It was okay, yes; it would be considered somewhat dumpy in the US, but he said it with pride, so I said, "Yes, very nice."

"That's right, this is very nice, for here. We didn't live like this when I was a kid, so yeah, it's different."

I had meant was the country different and started to reframe the question, but it was hot, we were both sweating, and I could tell he was thinking better of turning off the hose. "This heat," I said.

"The heat, yeah, that's the same now as then, I think, but you know, a kid— you don't know."

"Last week," I said, "I went to rent a car to go up north, and the guy at the Avis counter said, 'How do you like our climate? We have two seasons: hot and *really* hot. You came at the wrong time. This is the really hot one.'"

"Yeah," he said, looking off, thoughtful, then back at me, and to my surprise added: "Yeah. Sacramento sucks too."

It was turning evening, and as I was walking back to my hotel, I passed an empanada stand on the street. Four women sitting in plastic chairs around a spindly table told me I should order one. I said I would come back later. They ranged from around sixteen to fifty or so, and the youngest was rolling out dough. One in her twenties was filling pieces of dough and pressing the edges closed. The fiftyish woman was behind a cart, frying them.

"You'll come back later?" a forty-five-ish woman who wasn't doing anything said, and I focused on her. She had a floozy air, with the hair and makeup to match, had been sexy all her life and knew it, worked it, and was stone-hard except for a streak of whimsy. She said, "Uh-huh, you'll come later, uh-huh." This made the other women laugh. I wasn't sure what the joke was.

"Are you by yourself?" she asked.

"Yes," I said.

She raised a well-plucked eyebrow, and said, again, "Uh-huh. . . ." This made them laugh again.

Some neighborhoods in Manila, seedier than this one, reek of sex. The foreigners sit in bars and cafes between bouts nursing beers and coffees, and sometimes couples walk by, Euro man and Filipina, Chinese man and Filipina, on their way to hotel rooms. On a busy, club-filled avenue, a young girl in a small tight sleeveless dress sat on the sidewalk in front of me, and an older white man came up to her and said something. I couldn't hear what he was saying since his back was to me as I walked toward them. She shook her head—whatever he offered, she wasn't interested. As I approached, he leaned down to her, said something else. She looked at the street between her heels.

"I'm ladyboy," she said to him as I walked by.

"That's okay," the man said in an Australian accent. He appeared to be fifty-five; she, sixteen. "I like that."

"No, thank you," she said. "Not tonight. I'm tired. I'm going home."

I don't know what was said after that, but a half block later I turned around and saw that he was still leaning down, talking to her. She was still sitting on the curb. She looked worn out, head in hands, waiting for him to leave.

On the way back to my hotel, I came to my empanada stand, and the fiftyish fryer and the youngest women were still there, and they did not recognize me—which I knew because I said "I'm back!" and they looked confused. Another set of women were sitting with the young one at the table. I asked for an empanada, and the young woman handed me one. One of the new women at the table, who like the woman earlier was a fortyish wiseacre, asked me, with a wry smile and a twinkle, if I liked empanadas. I said yes and they all laughed. The young one, who was rolling and filling new empanadas by herself, didn't look up, but she chuckled too. The fryer stayed out of it.

"Yeah?" The funny one said. "You *like* our empanadas?"

"Yes, I *love* empanadas," I said—and I don't know why I said it with emphasis like that. It made them bust a gut laughing.

"You really like *our* empanadas, do you?" she said, still laughing.

"Well, I guess I don't know—I haven't tried yours yet," I said, starting to understand that "empanada" was a sexual innuendo, and as I ate one off a small tin plate—it was good, not great—I found myself asking, I don't know why: "What about you, do you like the empanadas too?" and now they laughed hard, looked at the woman this time, and even the fryer smiled.

"How did you know?" she asked, and they all laughed again. "You should have another. One good empanada deserves another, I always say! Have another!"

"Okay," I said, "I'll have another."

"Oh my, what a man! You want to eat another empanada?" she said, burlesquing the word now, while the young girl handed me a second. "That's right, she has a nice fresh one for you," she said, motioning to the youngest, "the freshest!"

They poked at the girl, who had already handed it to me, and laughed. I said thank you to the kid, who now seemed a little embarrassed. She was neither young enough nor old enough to find it funny. It can be very satisfying to offer yourself up as the scapegoat, as the butt of the joke, but I didn't like that they were teasing her too. The more they teased, the more she felt mortified.

The funny woman tried to get me to buy a third one, but I didn't. They weren't, as it turned out, that good.

"No," I said. "But thank you."

"Thank *you!*" she said. But she was done playing. She felt bad for the girl too, I thought, and the girl saw that and relaxed.

I left a tip—"Tank you," the fryer said—and then I walked slowly to my hotel, saw that the sun was gone, the night just waking up.

MONGOLIA

The twenty-story cranes were thick on the airport road, pulling rectangular apartment buildings up toward the sky, complexes of apartments propagating in thick patches, all the way from the airport to downtown. The road, only six miles long, often takes an hour, or two if it's raining or snowing, to navigate. The number of cars has increased by a factor of ten in just a few years, the lanes in the road hardly at all. The traffic is fierce, as are the drivers, squeezing in and out of lanes with careful, almost theatrical aggression. And just like in my home neighborhood of Silver Lake in Los Angeles, every other car is a Prius.

It's hard to think of Ulaanbaatar as a crossroads, because who would be crossing to where? And where would they be coming from? It isn't on the road to anywhere. It's more than six hundred miles to Beijing, the first big city to the southeast, eight hundred to Xining or 1,500 to Lhasa to the southwest, six hundred to Irkutsk in the north, which has only a half million people, and Ulaanbaatar has twice that. Due west there isn't anything for 3,700 miles, until you hit Moscow. Some of the caravans on what was known as the Tea Road from Beijing to Moscow passed through in the seventeenth century, but at that point Ulaanbaatar was less a city than a mobile caravansary, moving back and forth across the river, up and down its banks, not settling where it is now until well into the eighteenth century. It is at once both an ancient and a very new city.

I had picked, for my first night, not knowing where things were, a hotel on the edge of town and had to walk three or more miles to get to the center, to Sukhbaatar Square. On the way I saw huge banners draped down the sides of buildings, advertising a certain Sri Sri, with a three-story-high picture of a Jesus-lookalike South Asian guru, and in the square, men were setting up a stage, with towers of PA speakers and jumbotron screens on either side, and large portraits of Sri Sri everywhere. Aisles of plastic folding chairs were being lined up in front of the stage, row after row, seats for thousands, and I thought, wow, what kind of Quixotic project is this? How is this Sri Sri going to attract thousands of people to an event in a town square that, tourists and all, only had fifty or so people milling about at any time on a beautiful, cool but sunny Sunday afternoon in September, most strolling through on their way elsewhere or taking selfies with the mammoth statute of Chinggis Khan that adorned the front of the State History Museum on the plaza's north end. One kid circled lazily on a bike. The Sri Sri workers hived around the south end, festooning the stage, adding more chairs, running electrical cords and building yurts behind the speakers—dressing rooms? The workers outnumbered everyone else. This was the city at leisure, the way the community hung out, and it was quiet, almost empty. Besides, I thought, the Hindu guru was facing an uphill battle against the Buddhists, the secularists, and the shamanists that made up almost everyone I had met in the country.

I found a restaurant a couple blocks away that served milk soup with dumplings and watched another tourist—there weren't that many of us, and we stuck out—a few tables away as she was served a dish big enough to be a meal for four, constructed on top of a cleaved sheep skull. I smiled with a raised eyebrow and she laughed, clearly surprised by what had shown up at her table too. The rest of the diners were Mongolian families and groups of friends, members of what seemed a quite comfortable bourgeoisie. After my soup and a beer, I wandered the streets north of the square, hoping to find a camera store to replace a dead spare battery. No luck. North of the square was quieter, older, settled, and leafy—no high-rise cranes in those blocks—and as the sun lowered, I turned and headed back.

Entering the square, I saw that around big Chinggis it was almost as empty as before, with just a selfie now and then. But the south half of the plaza had filled up. Music was coming from the stage, and the thousand seats were full. Overflow people were laying out blankets around the edges—they had come equipped, knowing seating would be short. They were all being addressed by a man on the stage—not Sri Sri, but a Mongolian man, perhaps an emcee— speaking to them above the music. It was a holiday vibe, almost a music festival vibe, and indeed, a troupe of traditional musicians and singers came out in brightly colored lemon and blue and neon green silk frocks, traditional except some of the colors, with tall hats and a collection of stringed instruments. They started to play. Women sang into microphones, and the instruments had pickups. Then the men started throat singing, a style that sounds part didgeridoo, part gargling, and part falsetto, all coming from a single set of vocal chords at the same time.

Women on a long zither-like box and a Mongolian harp and men on a few two-string minicellos accompanied the singers as the last chairs were taken, and the overflow continued to converge.

Then Sri Sri, in long robes, long hair, and long beard, started to talk. He spoke in English, and a young Mongolian woman translated, each of them holding their own microphones. Sri Sri sat in a lotus, and she bent over reverentially, close behind.

"You please will close your eyes," he said, and thousands of Mongolians did. A three-count. "Breathe in deeply," he said, and then he did, held for a three- or four-count, and said, "Exhale."

Each of his statements was repeated, in the same soothing tone, by the translator. And he waited, calm, before saying, from the twin jumbotrons, "Feel your body."

And so, in a Guided Meditation 101, he relaxed the crowd and I took pictures. Thousands of Mongolians sat, eyes closed, some already looking blissed out. All were quiet.

"As your mind expands, your body recedes," he said. "As your body recedes, your mind expands."

The crowd soaked it up, and they all—the eighty-year-olds, the seventy-year-olds, the sixty-year-olds, the fifty-year-olds, the forty-year-olds, the thirty-year-olds—sat in meditative contentment, their eyes comfortably closed, their souls, or so it seemed, at happy peace.

After the meditation, hundreds of people walked up to the stage, across a gangway, and gave the guru a flower or just bowed. He smiled at each as they came up, and he touched some on the head. The music was loud again from the speakers, and the crowd was thrilled. The younger people ran around to get a closer look, while over the next hour the musicians left the stage, then half the large entourage, then Sri Sri, then the rest of the entourage. And then everyone slowly dispersed as the deep evening blue turned to gray.

Ulaanbaatar means "Red Hero." The city had been called Khüree (or Nomiïn Khüree or Ikh Khüree or Da Khüree or Bogdlin Khüree or Niïslel Khüree) for centuries, but it was renamed when the People's Republic of Mongolia was formed in 1924. Over the next half century, the People's Republic abolished religion, destroyed virtually all the temples in the country, murdered many tens of thousands of enemies of the revolution, collectivized agriculture, introduced extensive mining, and controlled culture and the press, most of this directed by Moscow. It wasn't until perestroika and glasnost that the country started to determine its own fate again.

The vast country is more than four times the size of Germany, with less than four percent of its population. Half of that three million people live in the capital, but about a million still live the life of the nomad. Imagine if, instead of the eight million people now living outside of Berlin in Germany there were only 250,000, and that they had sixteen million horses, sheep, camels, cattle, yaks, and goats. Multiply all that by four and you have Mongolia.

I met a woman working as a guide in UB at lunch one day, and she had a pronounced entrepreneurial streak.

"I am HR manager for mining company. Also project manager. Also manager," she said. This was before I realized that she only used the present tense and was talking about her early work life. "Big company, important company. But new election, new government, they make deal with China, kill company."

We were having lunch in a restaurant with traditional food, and she explained some of the dishes, looked after her charges for the day, two American women, but they didn't seem to have any questions for her, so she turned back to me.

"I have meat factory," she told me, "but government close it." Tens of millions of animals are slaughtered each year, and much of it goes to the export market, a central and significant contributor to the nation's economic well-being. The government, she claimed, has close ties with or outright owns all seven of the large meat processing plants, and they did not want her competition. She got the company up and running anyway, and three years in she had fifty employees. When it was clear she was successful, the government hassled her and fined her and took her to court, bleeding her until she lost it all.

"That is corruption," I said.

"It is over," she said, resigned. She wasn't happy, but she had moved on and was energetic and even-keeled. Now she wanted to start her own travel business. She didn't want to guide anymore, she said, she wanted to get married, raise a family, and stay in UB—no more living on the road. She knew this business now, she said, she could run it from home.

It struck me as I talked to her that the nomad families I had met were entrepreneurs too, each of them running a small animal husbandry business, managing their hooved inventory, expanding and contracting not just based on the grass but on the market. Another guide wanted to talk to me about setting up a website to go into business for herself, and a shaman I talked to wanted to write a book, but not just to write it—he wanted to publish it internationally. None of these people sounded like hustlers to me, they weren't grasping at pipe dreams or easy money. Nor were they looking for a job or a position. They had some entrepreneurial, expansive, world-creating trait that may just be profoundly ingrained in the culture, perhaps for no other reason than that the environment requires it. They love their herds and they love Chinggis Khan, who was, after all, a mergers and acquisitions guy, a hostile takeover specialist.

My guide down to the Gobi, Tsetseg, was a quick, personable, warm, and lovely person. Like my lunch companion, she had entrepreneurial ambitions and was anxious to get off the road. She had a teenage son who required her to have a few arguments on the phone during the trip, and a young daughter as well, who she missed when she was out guiding tourists on seven- and ten-day excursions around the country. Tourism employs a lot of people, almost all from UB, and they are made nomadic by their employment. But unlike the nomads, they cannot bring their families. The driver on my Gobi trip, Nandi, also had children, three school-aged kids. He shrugged when I asked whether he missed them, but to be fair he shrugged about most things. He was a chill guy, and he and Tsetseg shared jokes in the front seat. He had very little English but was enough of an empath to read what the tourists meant and needed most of the time.

The road leaving UB was a two-lane blacktop in good shape, and once out of the capital traffic, all was smooth sailing. Leaving Karakorum, though, the ancient capital of Chinggis Khan and his sons and grandsons, we split off to go to the Gobi, and the rest of the trip was on dirt paths and bits of gravel, bouncing in and out of ruts, crossing a stream here and there, not exactly off-road, but not exactly on a road either. Cellular coverage was faint and far between, and I realized the guidebooks were right—it would have been tough to go it alone. Gas stations were hundreds of miles apart, and when we happened upon a village, it certainly was not because there had been a single sign about it anywhere or any way to see it more than a few miles away. The tire tracks we were on, as in most places in the world with minimal roads, splayed off at times, and Nandi had to choose from among a dozen options, some of which devolved into foot-deep ruts left over from muddier days, some of which just wandered off toward a nomad's ger camp—"ger" being what the Mongolian yurt is called. Both Tsetseg and Nandi knew the country well, but even he had to back up a couple of times and try another path. And once they had to stop and call for guidance, although that was when they were looking for a particular nomad family's ger.

We had filled up with gas at a small village of the kind we had seen every hundred miles or so since Karakorum—a gas station, two mini-marts, a school, an agricultural warehouse, a dozen houses, three or four unidentified single-story buildings. "Mini-mart" is now almost as international as "okay"—I've seen it in dozens of countries—although in many places, as here, it is written in Cyrillic: мини-март. After an hour or so, we had peeled off the gravel road and followed tire tracks across the steppe, with a ger here and there and large herds of horses, sheep, and goats strewn across the endless, rolling green plains. A boy on a motorbike came out into this unmarked land to meet us. We saw him first in the distance, with a larger man riding on the back, both wearing big, traditional camel-hair coats. The older man hopped off and wandered away—where?—and left the boy to guide us into his family's ger camp. The boy was around twelve, it looked, and with a nod for us to follow he turned and started back. Herds of horses and herds of sheep and goats munched the green carpet that rolled out to the horizon.

We followed the motorbike a dozen miles overland, the boy showing us the best places to cross the stream in order to end up at his nomad family's camp for lunch. We were many miles from any road, and I again felt grateful that I was being driven around. I always opt for driving myself or using buses and trains when I can and only succumb when necessary. The guidebooks for Mongolia all said forget it, unless you are willing to carry not only spare tires and cans of extra gas, but tools for engine and suspension repairs too, and so I chose a tour company online and ended up being with a party of five: the guide and driver, two women from Virginia, and me. And one of the things Tsetseg and Nandi made possible was this meeting, and lunch, in the middle of nowhere. As I got out of the car to see my hosts milking their horses, a herd of animals along the horizon here and there, but no other sign of a living soul in any direction, I thought, not for the first time, this is the best of all possible worlds.

The steppe rolls, still green at the far end of summer, off the edge of the earth in every direction. Clouds give the sky depth. Flocks of giant birds migrate south. The sublime has never felt quite so earthbound, quite so mundane, quite so untamed and comfortable and beautiful.

Something happens between the guide and the tourist—and I realized that I had felt it before, in the hospital. An emergency room nurse had once helped me through a minor health crisis, and I couldn't help noticing, even while I was in the throes of extreme pain, that she was exquisitely competent—it shouldn't have been surprising, since it was all part of her job, I suppose, but she knew what needed to be done long before the doctor did, and she knew how to deal with both the practical realities and the emotional waves irregularly crashing into the emergency room shore. She was calm always, fast when she needed to be, but never hurried, and she had the gray hair, stolid body, and staunch confidence of someone who had seen all of this before and seen much worse. Once I had had my second shot of morphine and had gone from the blinding agony of the body in pain to the absolute bliss of morphine heaven, I turned to her and said, "It is so wonderful, what you do for people! It is just so wonderful!" And I loved her at that moment with a pure and total love.

In retrospect, there's a Stockholm syndrome aspect to the relationship—you relinquish control to the nurse, to the guide, and in putting yourself in their hands, some dynamic is formed that results in a feeling of great gratitude and respect. Not always; the FBI reckons that fewer than one in ten kidnapped people have this reaction to their captors, but with nurses and guides the relationship is, to put it mildly, less fraught, and therefore the syndrome must be much more common. I think back to the people who have helped me—the young man in Fez with the angelic voice, my rugby champion guide in Madagascar, the man who walked me around the Hittite ruins in Turkey, my driver in Bhutan, even the strange girl in Korea who didn't so much guide me as follow me around, and the strange sad young boy in Uzbekistan who showed me around the market—and in each case I ended up feeling something deep about them, feeling profound gratitude, not least because in each case I felt cared for, taken care of, protected, enveloped in a bit of a cocoon. For someone used to being alone on the road, fending for oneself day in and day out, this care can feel like a deep bath, a warm bed. Perhaps with a couple shots of morphine I would have declared my love to all of them.

Part of each of these relationships is a mind meld—the guide reads the tourist and the tourist reads the guide—and whatever the verbal interchanges, the non-verbal sense of being in it together, of unfolding a world together, of sharing wonder, is combined for the tourist (or the patient) with the feeling of surrender, and that combination of submission and intense mirroring is something that otherwise only happens, I realized, in the most intimate relationships in one's life.

My guide to the Gobi was involved in this kind of empathetic exchange in a different way too. She was interested in shamanism. She practiced a number of Buddhist rituals—she spun the prayer wheels at the temples, for instance—but she was much more interested in the religious and spiritual understandings that predate the introduction of Buddhism, the shamanistic practices that managed to survive when religious observance was banned by the Stalinist government. I stopped once and picked up a pretty piece of pink quartz as we were walking, and she told me to put it back. It is a terrible karmic mistake, she suggested, to take anything from nature as a trophy. It was just a small stone in an ocean of small stones, but okay, at some fundamental level she was right. Don't take what you don't need.

At one of the museums, there was a display on shamanism, with a life-sized shaman statue wearing a woven, beaded headdress that covered his face.

"I talked to a shaman in Southern Africa once," I told her, "and he had the same headdress." I thought this was a remarkable coincidence. She did not seem surprised.

I also talked about Mark Plotkin's book, *The Shaman's Apprentice*, which describes his years studying with a shaman in southern Suriname, learning all the Amazonian plants and substances used for cures and potions.

"Yes," she said. "But it is not just medicine. It is knowledge. It is the hidden world. The shaman has access to spirits."

The next day, we stopped at a temple complex that had been destroyed by the People's Republic. In the early twentieth century there were some hundred thousand monks in Mongolia, which was a remarkable 10 percent of the total population, and more than a thousand monasteries. Starting in the 1920s, religious practice was forbidden and monasteries closed. And then, in a few short years in the 1930s, under the direction of Stalin, some thirty thousand monks were killed, and mass graves containing hundreds of skulls with bullet holes through the back continue to be uncovered on former monastery sites. At least seven hundred monasteries were destroyed. Others were turned into museums and schools and housing.

"I want you to talk to my shaman when we are back in UB," she said. "I think he would be interested to talk to you. And I think you would be interested to talk to him."

"Does he speak English?"

"I can translate."

After I returned to California, I had dinner with a friend from Hungary. I told her about my trip and mentioned the great herds of horses on the steppes.

"Yes, those are our horses," she said.

"They what?"

"Yes, the Mongols, they stole horses from us in Hungary. That is why they have such good horses."

"Are we talking about the thirteenth century?" I asked, and she laughed.

"Yes, but still, they are our horses."

I told her about the lunch I had at the ger in the middle of the country, halfway between UB and the big dunes of the Gobi Desert, the one the young boy guided us to on his motorbike. The materfamilias slaughtered a sheep and made the national dish, which is sheep cooked with hot stones and root vegetables on the wood stove, the stones sizzling as she pulled them from the red coals in the stove and layered them among the meat and vegetables. While it was cooking she went out to milk the horses again, something she did seven times a day in the summer, five times a day in the fall. After lunch, she made vodka, building a little stovetop still and boiling fermented mare's milk until she had a pint or so of warm, crystal-clear vodka, which she melted butter in. In the midst of all this traditional activity, not that different from what could have happened a hundred years earlier, or, for that matter, in the thirteenth century, there were still signs of modernity. The family had a cell phone, though it only got a signal once in a while and only in one spot. They had a small solar panel that charged a car battery, which in turn could run a small TV from a satellite dish, and a small Bluetooth speaker that her twelve-year-old son played for his eighteen-month-old nephew to dance to. There was even a small washing machine they could haul the battery out to for clothes washing.

"Is that right?" my Hungarian friend said. "Did the washing machine say 'Made in Hungary' on it? Maybe they stole that too."

I had been amazed, through the whole trip, how omnipresent Chinggis Khan was, how alive that thirteenth-century history was for people. Now I know they are not alone. My friend was smiling, it was a joke—she didn't really think the washing machine sitting in the wilds of the Mongolian steppe was stolen from Hungary—but the animus was real. Her outrage at the Mongol invasion may have been exaggerated for comic effect, but we know about jokes, don't we. . . .

The invasion of Hungary in 1241 was, in fact, quite brutal. Somewhere between half and four-fifths of all Hungarian villages were destroyed, and as much as a quarter of the population, some half million people, were slaughtered. When Pope Innocent IV wrote to Güyük Khan in 1245, he was referring in part to the Hungarians when he rebuked him:

> We are driven to express in strong terms our amazement that you, as we have heard, have invaded many countries belonging both to Christians and to others and are laying them waste in a horrible desolation, and with a fury still unabated you do not cease from stretching out your destroying hand to more distant lands, but, breaking the bond of natural ties, sparing neither sex nor age, you

rage against all indiscriminately with the sword of chastisement.

Güyük's reply, a copy of which is in the museum in Kara-korum, is a priceless bit of table-turning. He suggests the Pope "and all the Princes" must immediately come to Mongolia and submit to the Khan, that they needed to promise to be obedient and pay homage. If you don't, he writes, "we shall know that you are our enemies." He mocks the Pope's assumption that he knows what God wants: "How do you think you know whom God will absolve and in whose favor He will exercise His mercy? How do you . . . dare to express such an opinion?"

And here, eight hundred years later, my Hungarian friend still resents the Mongol sword of chastisement.

"This was not right," she said, as if it were seven hundred and fifty years more recent, "what the Mongols did."

When we came across an *ovoo*, one of the heaps of sacred stones that are found at the tops of hills, at significant spots, in sacred places, with a stick in the middle tied with ribbons or prayer flags, Tsetseg walked around it three times, adding to a stone to the pile each time.

"Always in the direction of the clock," she said. "And you pray about the past as you go around once and throw one stone; then second time, the present; then third stone, the future."

I started doing it after that, especially if I ran across an ovoo when I was off on my own. Like many rituals, it had a soothing effect, and besides, it was what my guide wanted us to do. And I needed to do what my captor wanted.

I happened to be writing a short book at the time, *Aimlessness: An Introduction*, and in it I discussed a famous book of French theory, *A Thousand Plateaus*, by Gilles Deleuze and Félix Guattari. That book espouses what they call "nomadology," a way of thinking that refuses fixed points in favor of flux, that affirms fluidity in all things. They had an idealized image of what nomadism meant—idealized in its freedom and in its violence, like a Hollywood Western—and I found myself getting more and more irritated with them. I started talking to them in my head, saying *I am at nomadic ground zero, I am having lunch with nomads and dinner with nomads, and I can tell you, you don't know what you are talking about*. This was madness of course, since they are both dead, and because the theory is flexible enough to undermine my fixed resolve to dismiss it.

But how, finally, do we reconcile the world of ideas with the world of horses patiently being milked, with the practical wisdom of the big-shouldered woman who milked them, with the heat-seeking anger of my Hungarian friend, with my guide's guileless shamanism? I lay in my ger—I stayed at ger camps across the country—one night typing on my laptop, and then, stepping out into the frozen night, the moon that had shone on Chinggis Khan now shining on my own little patch of the interminable frosted ground, I wondered, how will I explain this moment? Smoke from wood stoves disappeared in the wind, the world asleep, the horses huddled against the night, no marauders within many days' drive. No Mongolian would steal a Hungarian's horse tonight. No French philosopher could turn this moonlit steppe, with all the earnest little gers clinging to its surface, into an idea. All was safe and sound. I ducked back inside, shuddered once at the cold, closed the computer, and slept until the first of dawn.

MICRONESIA

United Airlines flight 155 is more like a bus than a plane. No frills, the cabin beat up, seats a little stained and dingy. It leaves from Manila and touches down in Guam and a half dozen other spots before hitting Honolulu, skirting the top row of tiny Pacific islands just barely poking up from the ocean floor. It lands on each airstrip, drops off a few passengers and picks up a few, many wearing leis on their heads and around their necks, bestowed by their families at the airport. Almost everyone is in flip-flops, and there are more plastic bags and boxes tied with string than suitcases, more sarongs than slacks. Most people are hopping one or two stops, and the plane is on the tarmac for at most an hour. It's a bus with wings.

The flight runs Monday, Wednesday, and Friday, so a layover means two or three days in each spot. Some of these islands are so small that you can walk around them several times in two days and feel as if you've met a significant part of the population.

I landed in Weno, one of the islands in Chuuk Atoll, also known as Truk. Online, I had found three options for hotels—a new motel near the airport, an older two-story motel called the Truk Stop, and a lodge at the end of the island, the Truk Blue Lagoon, catering to divers. The airport motel was depressing, the Truk Stop was full, and so I booked a room at the Blue Lagoon on my phone.

I found a taxi at the airport driven by a man of about forty, energetic, wearing shorts and a faded T-shirt. The ride took almost an hour because the first section of road was under construction, down to one lane, much of it covered in mud soup, in some places more than a foot deep, and traffic was stopped for long periods to let backhoes and trucks through. The road was being built by a Japanese company, and most the equipment was driven by Japanese guest workers, with a handful of Micronesians doing things like directing traffic.

People hung outside a faded, frill-less supermarket, and the few other buildings were also bare, unadorned, and a bit run-down. The Truk Stop, when we passed it, looked significantly less impressive than it had online, where it didn't look that impressive. The beach was never far from the road, and the plant life was lush, the palms tall.

A mix, then, right from the start: mostly paradise, but here and there a garbage dump—trash, shacks, plastic blowing by, unmistakable poverty.

The driver and I talked about where we were born, our families. He had four kids.

"The boy's seventeen," he said. "The girl's twelve, the other boy's ten, other girl's eleven."

"Are they in school?"

"Yes, they both in school."

"So life is good here, or life is hard?" I asked.

"Life is good, little hard."

"It doesn't look like people have much money."

"If people work, money. If I don't work? No more

money for kids. Work, money." For him, his shrug suggested, it was a simple equation.

"Is there enough work for people who want it?" I asked.

"Yes. Most. Almost."

"Do you feel like things change here, or do they stay the same?"

"Oh now, things change—this road? Was very bad. Plenty muddy."

"Plenty muddy," I said.

"Oh, yes! Plenty! Now fixed. Before that? No change. Same."

"And that is good."

"Good. Okay. You business?"

"I'm a writer."

"Oh, because if you business, I help."

"Okay, thanks, but no, I am just here for a couple days, writing."

"Because I want to do business," he said. "Very much. I like to do business for future. You know the problem: money."

"Yes, you need capital."

"Yes, need money. This is my dream. I do business."

"What sort of business."

"Cigarettes."

"Cigarettes?"

"Yes, because, you know, that's fast! Cigarettes."

I was stumped. He looked over at me.

"Really fast!" He said. "Good business."

"Selling to shops or to people?"

"Shops?" He thought a minute. "Maybe to people. But! If a store want to buy from me, okay, I sell."

"Is there a cigarette tax?"

"Tax?"

"A special tax on cigarettes?"

"Oh, yes," he said. He had not thought about this.

"Might be a problem, maybe you need a license?" I said.

"Yes, problem," he said, thinking.

"The government here—it is good?"

"No. This road? They don't fix for long, long time."

But he was caught up, for the moment, thinking about the cigarette tax. He dropped me at the Blue Lagoon and gave me a card. This was normal—cab drivers most places give you a card to call if you need a ride. But this was his other card, his business card.

"Maybe you have friends," he said, "who do business. They call me."

I checked in and started walking around the island. At the top of a hill I saw what looked like a small one-room church and a man raking the yard in front of it. I climbed up to talk to him. There was a house behind and to the side of the rough-hewn church.

He was tall for an islander and had kind eyes. He was around thirty, with a soft speaking voice, wearing flip-flops and shorts. He said, "Please, come inside the church, I will get my father." The church was built by hand, partially open to the elements, and could fit as many as fifty or sixty people. Some sunlight came in between the walls and the eaves, and the windows had no glass, just shutters. It would have made Martin Luther happy—very little ornamentation, just a cross on the wall behind the altar, which was nothing but a plain table.

The father came in, wearing thin gold wire-rim glasses. He had some somewhat unkempt curly gray hair and whiskers—not at all clean cut and prim looking, but innocent as a kitten, and eager to please. He was very happy to see me, and his son was too. They never had strangers visit, they said, they just served the local people.

"You see it is a steep climb," the father said.

"Yes, we are not close enough to the road for tourists," said the son.

"And yet we are a church from strangers," the father said.

"A church from strangers?" I said. "Oh, of course. Missionaries."

"Yes, Church of Christ," the father said. "And a tourist translated the Bible." He smiled, full of wonder.

That stymied me. "A tourist?" I asked.

"Yes," the son said. "A British man, before I was born. He write the Bible in Trukese."

"He was a tourist?"

"Yes," the father said. "From England. He asked if we have Bibles and I say no. I was very young. He say, you build church, I write Bible."

"How long did that take?" I asked.

"The church?" He pushed his glasses back up his nose.

"Well, yes, but I meant the Bible."

"One year," the father said. "One year we have church and Bibles. He send from England. Enough for everyone."

The son excused himself to finish raking the lawn. The father and I smiled at each other, and I asked how he became a minister.

"We have a church and Bible, but no minister." He shrugged, as if to say he had no choice, and smiled. He didn't seem to feel it a burden.

Back down at the bottom of the hill, I walked further and saw a guy sitting on a rock in the shade, tapping a walking stick on the ground. He wore a Metallica T-shirt and no shoes. He was about my height, about my weight, maybe a little heavier, half my age.

We said hello, and then he asked if I was the one who had walked up to the church. I said yes, and I asked if he went to that church.

"No. Sometimes," he said.

"Life is hard here, it seems," I said, in part because he didn't seem particularly happy. Not miserable, just slightly defeated. I decided he was younger than I thought, some indeterminable age before thirty. He had a longish shock of black hair and the scarcest of beards.

"Yes," he said. "I drop out of school, and then things are hard."

"Are you married?"

"Yes, this is my wife's house," he said, pointing to the house right next to us on the road. I had seen a woman inside the open door with a few children. "My house is up there," he added, pointing farther up the hill.

"Your wife's house. So it is her family's house?"

"Yes, I born right up there," he said, again pointing up the hill. "She born here."

It didn't seem like the right thing to ask detailed questions about property rights and their relation to the kinship system, so I almost let it pass.

"So the husband moves to the wife's house?"

"Yes," he said, sounding as if I had dropped slightly in his estimation, not knowing that.

"The tourists who come here—that is a good thing, right, good for the economy?"

"Yes," he said. "Sometimes I get coconuts and tourists give me money. Sometimes I draw—how do say—to show where to go?"

"A map?"

"Yes, a map, for diving or for Japanese guns. The tourists pay for this, they collect — they collect them for souvenir, the map."

"And are there jobs, at the hotel, for instance?"

"Yes, there is job. But it is hard for me because I don't finish school."

"Can you go back?"

"Go back?"

"To school."

"Oh, no, I am old now ..."

"*I* am old, you are not old."

He laughed. "For school, yes, I am old. I am twenty-nine. This is my boy."

An eight-year-old in a pair of shorts had run up. I snapped a picture of them, showed them. The boy ran off.

"But you get by," I said.

"Yes, there is food here on the trees, that is good. We grow some things."

"What about clothes and medicine?"

"It's okay, we trade a little, take some to market, we get some money, we buy what we need, imported things, rice, cooking oil—it's okay."

"So what do you think will happen, in the future."

"The future?"

"Yes, for you."

He looked at the ground in front of his feet, tapped his stick, and took a minute.

"Things change," he said.

NICARAGUA

The largest sign visible from my hotel window in downtown Managua was bright red and backlit, with letters twenty feet high: SEMINOLE CASINO. It was built by the Seminole Nation of Florida under license from the Sandinista government. If there is a more bizarre symbolic clusterfuck of omnidirectional oppression, I haven't run into it. The Seminole tribe has since sold it.

The Sandinistas—the good-guy revolutionaries who liberated their country from banana republic puppets and dictators only to *Animal Farm* themselves almost instantaneously into klepto-autocrats—are responsible for opening their country to the notoriously dirty gaming industry. I would have thought that the socialist revolution had been betrayed enough by Daniel Ortega and his infamous shopping binges, but no—he decided to welcome the most exploitative, criminal-saturated business in the world into the heart of Managua. And that it carries the name of one of the tribes forced onto the Trail of Tears by Andrew Jackson only adds layers to the accretion of historical woe.

I asked Eduardo, the security guy at my hotel, about Ortega and the government, about why he kept getting elected. Eduardo had a shotgun over his shoulder at all times, riding on his bit of a paunch, and he was suitably alert, standing outside the front door. Armed guards were ubiquitous as I drove through Guatemala, El Salvador, Honduras, and Nicaragua in the last weeks, sitting on plastic chairs in front of shops and in parking lots, literally riding shotgun in delivery trucks, inside and outside banks and malls. Eduardo had a kind, responsive face and put up with my Spanglish, correcting me here and there (I kept pronouncing my *h*'s), and when I asked him what he thought, he said, "*No le busques tres pies al gato.*" It took a while, but I finally got it—"don't look for three feet on a cat," meaning something like "don't expect a zebra to change its stripes." Things are bad, people are afraid for their future, and the Sandinistas are good at scaring people, he said. Besides, he said, "*ellos engañan*": they cheat.

From my window I could also see one of the largest malls in Managua, Metrocentro, and having been on the road for several weeks, I needed a few things. I started to walk around dusk, and Eduardo said he would call a cab.

"But it is right there," I said, pointing. "Right?"

"Yes, best to take a cab."

I was used to people being overprotective and said I'd like to give it a try on foot. It was a quarter mile at most.

"I don't recommend it, sir." It was the first time he had called me *señor*, and I should have noticed.

"I'll take a little look and come back for a cab if it looks dicey."

He shrugged—*your funeral*, the shrug said.

It was late fall and getting dark fast. I walked to the end of the hotel drive and crossed the street, looking for the best route. The mall was right there, in sight. There was a four-lane road to cross without much traffic and then a small gulley, on the other side of which a narrow road headed to the parking lot. I couldn't see the whole route, but it looked quiet enough, simple enough, quick enough. I could taxi back.

By the time I crossed the road, though, it had fallen dark—I hadn't noticed the dark clouds gathering, and they had swallowed the last of the sun. I heard rustling in the brush below me. I felt more than saw bodies moving toward me from either side. A hand reached out of the darkness and grabbed my leg: a horror movie event. I shook my leg free, turned around, and dashed back across the road, weaving through the traffic. In the lights from the hotel I could now see that the people closing in on me from behind were kids, twelve, thirteen, fourteen, who looked hard and hungry. When we got to the lights from the hotel they stopped, shied away, and slunk back into the darkness.

Several guys were now in front of the hotel, including Eduardo and a cab driver, and they tried not to laugh at me but didn't do a very good job. I took the cab to the mall, and the driver talked merrily of *cuidado* and *peligro* and *niños malos*, and said he would wait for me.

The first thing I noticed inside the mall was that it was just a mall—the same shops, the same clientele as in Glendale or Sherman Oaks, and everyone blithely unaware, it seemed, of the desperation surrounding their bubble. Which wasn't true, of course—of course they knew, like the people at the hotel knew, like the cabbie knew. Thirty percent of the population lived on less than two dollars a day. Desperation was everywhere. Just not in the mall.

When I came out with my bag of toothpaste and water and other things I could have done without, my cabbie was waiting for me and waved.

The next day, I had a long conversation with a man in a little lunch place about Ortega. When Ortega had been part of the ruling junta that overthrew the dictator Somoza in 1979, he had been responsible for cutting child mortality and illiteracy in half in just a few years. He was a hero of the fight against American imperialism, pushing back the Reagan-backed Contras in the 1980s and protecting the power of the Nicaraguan people. He was so popular that he won the first free and fair elections in half a century in 1985 with 67 percent of the vote. He was applauded at home and overseas.

By the fortieth anniversary of the deposing of Somoza, he was a classic dictator himself, scrapping laws that limited his power, treating the national treasury like his own patronage fund, jailing and torturing journalists, organizing election fraud at every level, corrupting the courts, and removing term limits to allow him to be elected for four new five-year terms.

"How," I asked the man sitting next to me, in my bad Spanish, "how he does go so bad so fast?" Getting the tenses right is not my strong suit. "How does he happen?"

"This is normal, isn't it?" he said. "Everywhere. Power corrupts. He now has absolute power. And corruption always has many friends."

"And do the people think with you? Or is he popular still, true?" It was my attempt to ask whether he was still truly popular or whether the election figures, which had him winning last time with 72 percent of the vote, were as ginned up as people said. He was kind and rephrased my questions, spoke slowly and watched to see if I was understanding.

"Many people in the countryside don't know any better, and—do you notice?—now he is a big Catholic, almost as big as the pope! People like that. The Catholics like it. The evangelicals like it."

"People in the countryside have television, I see." Driving down from Honduras to the capital, I had clocked satellite dishes on the smallest of ramshackle houses. "They get news, right?"

"He and his friends own all the TV stations. He kills journalists who tell the truth." He shrugged, held out his hands.

"You sound"—I said and paused, not finding the word for resigned—"*resignación*?"

"*Renunciada*, yes, resigned to our fate. I think we who remember the revolution"—he was in his sixties—"we think, okay, we had our chance, we did it, and then this is what happens, so what can we do? Have another revolution, bring a new Ortega to the front? What would be the point?"

A few people near us listened in now and then, sometimes nodding in agreement. This was a small neighborhood place that didn't see a lot of gringos, so people were eavesdropping at first and then joined the conversation, agreeing with a word or gesture or grunt.

"You have no—*esperanza* means hope, yes?—you have no hope?"

"*La esperanza*? Maybe. Or *la ilusión*." I looked it up later, *esperanza* is hope, but *ilusión* can also mean hope—or delusion, hallucination. "One day, he will die and maybe we will have a chance again. We don't know. Nobody knows."

An old man at the next table looked at him and nodded. "*Si*," he said. "*Nadie sabe*."

KAZAKHSTAN

W here are you going?" the man I met on the street in Almaty asked me when I said I planned to see some of the rest of Kazakhstan. We were talking in a stately park with old trees, still with a coating of frost in early spring. Almaty is the country's largest city, with some late nineteenth- and early twentieth-century buildings, like the storybook yellow-and-green Zenkov Cathedral, as well as some Soviet-era big blocks and some later, oil-boom showcases built before the capital moved to Astana (now Nur-Sultan) in the late 1990s. Nur-Sultan, the second biggest city, has half the population of Almaty. The rest of the country is sparse—only eight of the 230 countries in the world are larger than Kazakhstan, and only fifteen are less dense. I really did want to know where he thought I should go.

"First I was thinking Shymkent," I said, "and then Turkistan."

"Shymkent is the south of Kazakhstan—different people," the man said. "We call them Texas." He smiled, as if to say, this is both silly and apt. He shot a couple of air-six-shooters. He was sixty or so, relaxed in his own skin, wearing a wool topcoat and a hat with the earflaps turned up. He let me take his picture and was neither pleased nor displeased with the results.

"But they are Kazakhs, just like you, right?"

"Kazakh is not Kazakh," he said. "There are many nations, over one hundred nations."

"You mean like Russians, Uzbeks?"

"No. Yes, there are many Russian, and there are Uzbek, Kyrgyz, Ukraine, Georgia, Chechen, everyone. But no, Kazakh is many tribes: Alban, Shapyrashty, Argyn, Kipchak, many, many. A shitload, you say, yes?"

He had a barrel chest and an air of kindly, bemused, but unquestionable authority. I had thought, for a minute, that he might be a spy in the security services, chatting me up to see if I might be trouble for the regime. He looked like the guy in the spy films who you can't tell is good or evil but ends up being evil. Then I decided he couldn't be a spy because he wasn't interested enough in me, didn't ask any more questions. Plus, he let me take his picture, which, unless he was planning to kill me, would have been a bad spy move. Also, shitload of ethnic groups? They must have a better spy school than that.

I asked him if he was a spy. He laughed.

"Close. I am police, I am cop." He was smart, plenty smart enough to be a good cop, plenty smart enough to be a bad cop. "But I retire. Now, peace!"

I asked how he felt about his government.

"Good," he said, in a uninflected, noncommittal way.

Nursultan Nazarbayev, the autocratic, often brutal strongman, has ruled the country since independence. Although he is no longer president, he is still one of the world's longest-ruling terroristic strongmen. In 2019, he created a "security council" that has ultimate authority over the president and parliament, which the parliament ratified as a constitutional amendment. He then had himself appointed Chairman for Life of the council, and he stepped down as president. On the recommendation of this new security council, the capital, Astana, was renamed Nur-Sultan in his honor, as if Donald Trump had renamed Washington, DC, Don-Ald. While Nazarbayev was setting up his new governmental system, an opposition newspaper reported that he had, over the preceding decades, secreted a cool billion dollars of state funds in a Swiss bank account. A decapitated dog was left in the lobby of the paper's offices, with a note saying "there will be no next time," and the head of the dog was dropped on front steps of the editor's home. Then the offices were firebombed. Torture of political dissidents is common.

"People outside don't like him, Nazarbayev," I said. "But people inside, I have heard, like him a lot."

"Outside? Where is outside?"

"The US. The UK."

He shrugged.

And then I remembered what my guidebook had said and told him. "I read that people don't like to talk politics here."

"No," he said, just the way he said "good," waving me off and changing the subject. "First time in my country?"

"Yes," I said, "first time, and first day."

"Welcome," he said. "First time in Muslim country?"

"No, North Africa, Middle East. And I've been to other places in Central Asia—Uzbekistan, Iran..."

"I am in Iran," he said.

He spoke English the way I spoke French and Spanish, all in the present tense.

"Very nice people, right? Warm. Hospitable." He raised an eyebrow at this last word, and I translated: "Friendly."

"Yes, yes, but, government, I don't like—dark. Dark ideology. Bad with women, covered—dark..."

"Agreed, but at least the women in Iran can drive. Saudi Arabia—"

He laughed. "Like, okay," he said. "But this is small potatoes, you say, yes? . . . Where else do you go?"

"Kyrgyzstan, Xinjiang, Turkey, Georgia, Azerbaijan, Armenia—"

"Okay," he said. "But Georgia, Azerbaijan, Turkey, Armenia—this is not Asia, this is Europe, this is NATO."

"Do you think there is a threat of what happened in Ukraine or Georgia happening here?" I asked. "Are people afraid of Russia taking back parts of the country?"

"No, people are not afraid . . . ," he said, but then he stopped himself and shook his head, smiling, a little laugh. He was genial about it, but he wasn't going there. A knowing smile said, *You read about it, so you know you shouldn't ask me to talk about politics.* . . . We had enough eye contact, though, to let me know that Russia was not at the top of the list of things to worry about, that Nazarbayev was, and I knew that he knew that I knew— we had just discussed politics without discussing it, and he understood that his silence was a message. Maybe it wasn't a clear message, but it was clear enough. "It's a politic!" he said, shrugging.

We talked about what else he thought I should see, and then, before long, without thinking, I made the same mistake.

"You are old enough, I think, to remember the Soviet Union," I said.

"Of course."

"How was that?"

"Not bad." He again looked me in the eye.

"It's a politic," I said smiling.

"Yes!" he said. "You see the cathedral?" It was just down the road, the outside freshly painted, not quite gingerbread, but elaborately trimmed, the steep spire and exterior the brightest yellow and white and green, the inside gold and silver, and I had spent the morning there listening to a remarkable choir.

"I was there this morning, people were singing, beautiful harmonies, and astounding acoustics, wow."

He was trying to decide whether he cared to have any of the words I just used translated, decided against it.

"You go to Wild West," he said, and shook my hand. "You will like."

He turned up his collar and continued his stroll.

I could never decide why he didn't mention the Nauruz celebrations that were just then happening all over the country. Nauruz (or Nowruz, Novruz, Navrus, or Nauryz) is the vernal equinox celebration that is observed across Western Asia, Central Asia, Iran, Northern India, Bangladesh, the Caucasus, the Black Sea countries, and the Balkans. It is also New Year's in Iran and Afghanistan. As I left him, I walked into a more commercial part of the city, where in front of a recently built mall, a yurt was set up on a small plaza, and some young women in colorful traditional dress—with tall, fairytale conical hats, wearing lime and red silk dresses—were milling about handing out flyers. They didn't speak much English, but they pointed to a sign that read Наурыз. I could sound it out and looked up Nauruz and Almaty on my phone. The celebrations ran for four days, starting that day. Why hadn't anyone mentioned it? My hotel was a gray ex-Soviet affair, with customer service to match, so not surprising, but why hadn't my cop mentioned it? I suppose if I met a tourist on Christmas Day in New York, I might assume that of course the tourist knew it was Christmas and maybe wouldn't say anything—and besides, what if they're Muslim or Jewish? Wouldn't it be rude?

Once I was attuned to it, I recognized signs everywhere. I should have noticed.

I flagged a cab and said, "Nauruz?" He nodded and drove for twenty minutes straight north, far out of the city, far enough that I started to wonder if we were on the same page, but a few minutes later, we were in the thick of it. Most of the city had converged on the fairgrounds, and people in traditional dress, camels in fancy saddles with holiday tassels, and horses in medieval drapes were everywhere. I paid the cabbie and walked in. It was bustling like a state fair midway, with a bit of jostling, families eating snacks and meat on skewers, impromptu food stands lining the walkways, some with small charcoal barbecues, some with larger rigs billowing smoke, pots issuing steam.

I followed the largest stream of people to an oval track with twenty rows of bleachers on one side, where a horse race was underway. The jockeys were kids as young as six or seven, the oldest eleven or twelve, on full-size horses that were galloping at breakneck speed, the enormous animals, muscles gleaming, making the kids look even smaller. Saddleless, bareback, with the reins in one hand and a short riding crop in the other, they whacked their horses' backsides and turned to see who was gaining on them, the horses thundering by thirty or forty strong, going around and around a mile-long oval, dirt flying up from their hooves. This was not the standard mile or mile and half American horse race; it was many miles long, and who knew how many times they had gone around before I got there? The horses were already lathered and the tiny jockeys already red-faced when I first saw them. A few more times around the track, a ten-year-old won, flagged by the horseback referees, and he thrust his crop in the air while trying to slow down his glistening steed, the horse still fiercely competitive. The the rest of the boys, smaller than their horses' necks, were still straining forward to try to place. I couldn't help imagining an American parent—or an American attorney—watching in absolute horror, imagining broken backs and trampled young bodies, as these kids flew by with nothing to hold onto except, when they needed to, their horses' manes.

After the race, other boys stood with their birds of prey, some of the birds looking almost as big as the eight- and twelve-year-old boys who had them perched on a leather glove, and a new competition was started. A boy would unhood his bird and let it fly. A man galloped by on a horse, dragging a freshly killed hare on a thirty-foot rope, and the eagle would dive at it and bring the kill back to its diminutive master. That was followed by an archery competition in which men on horseback galloping at full speed inconceivably hit three targets in a row, pulling fresh arrows from a quiver on their back.

In the middle of the track, teenagers in traditional dress, making them all look like Aladdin and Mulan, perched on steeds in their fancy costumes, waited for some other competition or performance, and they gladly posed for me and my camera. The competitors—or performers—were in pairs, boy and girl, and they clearly knew each other, leaning against their partners without getting off their horses. They lounged with the confidence of Taylor Swift in her dressing room, belles and beaus of the ball all.

The twenty rows of bleachers, 150 yards long, were full to bursting with people of all ages. After the archery was over, a new competition started, in which riders galloping down the track leaned to the ground, trick-riding off the side of the horse, almost upside down, with one foot in a stirrup, the other foot holding on to the top of the saddle, their heads inches from the furious hoofs, and picked up a series of cloth wads, tossing them to the side. Some managed to grab one or two, a couple got six or so, but only one rider managed all eight. He was in a bright yellow traditional outfit, riding a white horse, and when he came to the center stage to pick up his prize, he looked not quite real, just like the Disney princes and princesses in center field, as if he were playacting, which of course to some extent he was. Like professional sports around the world, it is both competition and entertainment, and when the players look like movie stars—did I mention that the princes and princesses were very beautiful?— the entertainment function lurches to the front.

When the trick riders were done, the princes and princesses approached the track, and two rode to the far end, each boy lined up a horse length or two behind a girl. A referee on horseback, a solid man of sixty, built like a weight lifter, set them off by dropping a flag. They burst into a gallop, the boy trying to catch the girl, while the girl took turns whipping her horse and whipping the approaching boy as he tried to grab her. When he did, he clutched her around the waist, pulled a handkerchief out of her shirt and waved it victoriously to the crowd, which cheered, and then he leaned in, both riders thundering down the track side by side, and to give her an unwanted kiss on her cheek. In return, she gave him a good smack on the face, hard enough to make him whelp, and the crowd cheered and laughed again. When he did manage to force a kiss on her mouth, standing up in his stirrups, no hands on the reins, both horses at top speed, the crowd roared again—the most cheerful rape-culture drama ever displayed to a daytime family audience.

Then, after a dozen boys had chased and manhandled and forcibly kissed a dozen girls down the track, one by one the couples raced back the other way, except this time the man had a full horse's length head start, and when the woman caught up with him she swung at him, smiling enthusiastically, with her whip. He tried to avoid the hits by hanging off the far side of his horse, his head almost on the ground as his partner leaned across his saddle to beat him about the ass and legs. Again, the crowd lit up in laughter and cheered whenever a blow landed with a resounding whack.

I had been getting closer and closer to the action with my camera and had wandered into the infield—nobody stopped me or seemed concerned, as it is clearly not a culture afraid of a little physical harm or of a little rule-breaking. Any one of the fifty ten-year-olds racing without saddles or helmets or the dozens in these competitions could have been maimed for life, and I had already noticed that in everyday life small things like traffic laws or red lights were not observed either. There were plenty of police and army posted around the arena, but they paid me no mind. Perhaps I was allowed to stroll into the center of things unmolested because I was the only non-Kazakh person in the huge crowd. Perhaps I looked like a journalist? Or maybe anyone who wanted to could have the had same access. I took close-ups of all the competitors and stood next to the track for the runs; I did have a full-size camera, and I started to act like I was an actual photojournalist, suggesting that was why I was there. In any case, it worked.

The culmination of the day was a game of kokpar. Kokpar is a cross between polo and rugby, with the significant difference from both being that a goat is slaughtered for use as the ball. In American football, the ball is called a pigskin, but this is the goat skin, flesh, bones, and guts. A referee, also on horseback, drops the goat carcass in a circle in the middle of the field—around the size of football field—and then the five men on each team scrum, the horses jamming up against each other as the men lean off their horses and try to grab the dead goat off the ground, using their horses and their arms and whole bodies to try to push their rivals out of the way. A point is scored if someone manages to gallop down the field, over the goal line, and drop the goat in a five-foot circle chalked in the end zone. That didn't happen often—the scoring was more like a soccer match than a basketball game. As soon as someone had the goat-ball, all five men on the other team fought as hard as they could to wrestle it away. It was standard technique, it seemed, to tuck part of the goat under your leg once you had it, but it was still hard to hold on to, especially with several guys from the other team yanking on it.

I was frantically taking pictures, and at one point the writhing mass of ten horses—snorting and bucking and brawling, half of them pushing toward one end zone, the other half pushing in the opposite direction, evenly matched so that all they could do was move sideways—was headed straight at me on the midfield sideline. I was using a telephoto, and although I kept backing it off to keep the roiling mass of horseflesh and human flesh in the frame, I couldn't tell how close they were getting to me on the sideline. The pictures I was getting were so spectacular, though, that I couldn't bear to stop and look right at them without the viewfinder and gauge how much time I had to get out of their way. It occurred to me that this is how war photographers got killed, transfixed by the approaching danger, unable to stop snapping the shutter. Finally, I panicked and stepped to the side; the scrum slid over the line and broke up, because once the goat is out of bounds, it is dropped back in the circle, where, once more, the battle begins anew.

Once the game ended, some of the young riders were showing off for each other, but the official competition was over. People had food stalls along the main routes in and out of the fairgrounds, small barbecues set up for skewers of shashlik, others selling drinks and snacks and sweets. Again, like the midway at any state fair, it was jammed with families and teenagers, the little kids running around like maniacs, the teens checking each other out surreptitiously. I decided to get some of whatever they were grilling before heading back to the city and patted my pocket for my mound of cash—it's one of those countries that haven't kept up with their own inflation, so a hundred dollars' worth of tenge makes a pile over an inch thick, twice that folded. I had two hundred bucks because I had just arrived, and I had split it into two piles to carry in two different pockets, partly for the bulge, partly a reflex traveler's precaution, and as I started slapping them all—I had pants with extra pockets, a shirt with pockets, a jacket with pockets, and I went around the horn a couple of times, trying to remember where I had put the bills. I started to feel an odd panic: I'd been pickpocketed! The cash was nowhere, none of it. All those frolicking kids bumping into me as I strolled, all those sweet people smiling as I walked by, while some delinquent had been pulling out my cash.

When I first arrived at the festival, everything was so chaotic, so crowded that I was not paying attention, and I thought yes, a perfect setup—a noisy spectacle, me besotted, me as Candide, as Quixote, in love with what is in front of my eyes as the world plots behind my back, wandering like a trusting idiot, alone, such a beautiful target, solo, nobody watching my back. I did see a few other non-Kazakhs during the day, most Chinese, but one European-looking family. And then me, the stupid American with the wads of cash bulging out of his pockets, which ones he didn't even know. I luckily had a few American twenties in my hat for emergencies, so I grabbed a cab and asked him to wait while I changed one at the hotel when we got there.

I went up to my room with that bereft feeling that this world I had made up for myself, this world full of kind strangers, was all a lie, that everywhere I went people were friendly because I was more likely than the next person to give them money or buy them a meal or hire them or help them get a US visa. Or let them pick my pockets. It was all a massive self-delusion—the idea I could have thought that my goal was the accidental intimacy of the road! What hogwash! What a fool.

I went up to my room, and to top things off, even though I had been gone all day, nobody had come to straighten the room, the bedclothes still in my jet-lagged, twisted mess, no fresh water, nothing. And that's when I saw on the table the two piles of cash. I had taken them out when I arrived at the hotel and never put them back in my pockets. And then, as if watching the security tapes, I saw, in my mind's eye, the maid coming in, starting to do her work, seeing the two piles of cash and thinking, *no way am I getting accused of lifting any of this numbskull's money*, and I imagined her backing out of the room like a cartoon character—better to say she had never entered, she had just missed that room, than to be forced to explain that she hadn't touched the piles. . . .

I felt terrible for making her deal with this, for laying her in the path of temptation like that, for carelessly leaving however many weeks or even months of her salary sitting next to my shaving kit like it didn't matter, like it was peanuts. I wasn't Candide, I was some minor demon. And to think I had broadcast suspicion and fear across the crowd just minutes before.

At least, I comforted myself, I didn't have to abandon my general theory of human goodness, however much I had to fall on that scale in my own estimation.

Nauruz lasts for four days, so when I got to the small city of Turkistan on the express bus, I was in time for their biggest day. Turkistan was the home of Khoja Ahmed Yasawi, a poet and mystic who was central to the development and spread of Sufism in the twelfth century, who I had never heard of until I read up on Turkistan that week. His mausoleum, a dozen miles from the center of town, is the architectural, historical, and spiritual jewel of the city, and when I arrived, a Nauruz festival was underway on its extensive grounds. Young women in fantastical traditional dress, representing each of the various tribes the ex-cop told me about—what he had called the shitload of various tribes—posed for pictures, and families ate from food stands or large yurts that had been set up for the occasion.

When you buy a ticket to the mausoleum, you get a guide, and mine was an impressive young woman in a full conservative headscarf, who had studied English and history and took me, object by object and year by year, through the museum and Ahmed Yasawi's life. She liked her job as a guide but wasn't done learning, she made clear—she wanted to go back to school. She was determined to be a professional historian; she loved history.

"Follow me," she said, and started explaining the place room by room.

Her English was superb, and when I asked, she talked about the two English teachers who had taken an interest in her. They had practiced with her after school and pushed her to read their English-language books and magazines, all from the US and UK. She knew all along, she said, that she was a nerd, that the other kids thought she was a nerd, but she felt fine about that. She was interested in Yasawi's monastic life not just because he was important—he founded a major religion!—but because she felt that her own inclination was to quiet study. Some of her classmates hated being alone, hated reading, hated theology—they all were religious, they would *say*, but they didn't really think about it, they weren't really consumed by it—and so she knew she was different. She loved reading and thinking, loved philosophy and religion and history, and was happiest when she was reading. We bonded on that—I told her I was the same, I had devoted my life to reading and writing. I wasn't sure about the monasticism, but all the rest of it, yes.

"Did you know," my guide asked me, "the age of the Prophet when he died?"

"The Prophet Muhammed?"

"Of course the Prophet Muhammed," she said. We were walking across the main room of the mausoleum. "He died at sixty-three. And Ahmed Yasawi, when he turned sixty-three—"

"Khoja Ahmed Yasawi?" I asked, because I wasn't sure I had heard right.

"Yes, Khoja Ahmed Yasawi. We call him Ahmed Yasawi. When he was sixty-three, he knew he did not deserve to be in the world longer than the Prophet, and so he dug himself a cave, and here"—she pointed to a hole in the floor with a railing around it that we were approaching—"under this monastery, he built this cave in his sixty-third year and entered it and never again came to the surface of the earth. He remained underground for the rest of his days, living in meditation and contemplation, never taking part in life aboveground, never again speaking to anyone. He spent sixty-three years underground in silent meditation and died in the year 616, or 1219 in your calendar."

"Wait, he lived . . ."

"Yes, he lived to be 126 years old, sixty-three years aboveground, and sixty-three belowground."

"I suppose this is possible . . ."

"Of course it is possible."

"And people brought him food, and . . ."

"People were very devoted to him; he was the greatest teacher in our tradition. Please follow me."

She took me to a room full of medieval swords and other weapons, and I tried a couple of times to return to the date of Khoja Ahmed Yasawi's death, but she avoided answering, not rudely, but like a teacher who knows the student will figure it out for themselves with another few minutes.

She was good at her job and kept the descriptions of things interesting, moving at a nice brisk pace. Many times, I've had a museum guide basically recite what was on the legends on the wall, but this guide was an actual historian, and she brought all her voluminous information to bear, animated by her love of the subject. I was a great audience, frankly, and I felt she appreciated my attention, my questions and comments, felt like we were in it together. At the end of the tour, she walked me outside and I gave her an oversized tip.

All around us the assorted bevies of young women in traditional garb were posing for pictures. Each cluster of six to ten women were dressed identically in striking, bright outfits—one group in lime green taffeta skirts with Kelly green velvet tops and eighteen-inch-high white turbans, edged with embroidery in yellow and green; another group was all in white, with embroidered filigree trim in red and green, and headgear that started as a cloche but ended in a tapering narwhal tusk or unicorn horn of white felt, sticking straight up to end in a plume of white feathers; a third posse wore pink frilly dresses with dark red tunics embroidered in white and gold, with thick fur hats that also had a spray of white feathers on top, and a pink Dutch Masters neck flounce edged in red.

They were stunning, beautiful, and had that deep glow young women get when they are dressed to the hilt and enjoying being the center of attention. Yes, my guide said, when I made a comment to that effect. But although they were very pretty, she pointed out, their costumes were not historically accurate.

"Speaking of which, listen," I said. "If you don't mind? I am a historian—I have written a number of books of cultural history—and I have a suggestion for you."

"Of course," she said, no more or less wary than anyone should be in the face of such an offer, which is to say a little wary. She knew she was a competent person who knew her stuff and was correspondingly confident, but I had just pulled rank with the "number of books" business, so she was a little suspicious—*mansplaining alert!*

"You are very good at this," I said, hoping to undo the damage but realizing as soon as it was out of my mouth that I was continuing to be patronizing. She heard it too, an eyebrow flinching for a microsecond. For some reason I noticed the headscarf I had long since forgotten, as if by breaking the implicit contract we had—that she was the local expert who knew better than the dumb tourist and got to tell me what was what—I had resurfaced our geopolitical differences and all they meant. We went from being people who had walked through history together for three quarters of an hour to people who had just met. I had turned her back into a stranger.

But it was too late to stop, or so it seemed. "Maybe, for people like me," I said, and again I realized too late that I sounded like a priggish know-it-all, but I couldn't just say "never mind," which would be just as bad, maybe even more patronizing, so I kept going. "Maybe if you just said 'people say' or 'he is recorded as dying sixty-three years later, at the age of 126,' it would be easier for us to accept."

"Yes," she said, with the slightest of smiles. "I understand."

She was very smart. She wouldn't argue.

I could see she pitied me.

As I took pictures of the groups of costumed women, I realized that I had noticed subliminally, but hadn't quite thought through, that the women in Kazakhstan look *right* at you. In the US and many other places, if a man catches a woman's eye, just out walking or in a restaurant, the woman will drop her gaze, pretend not to notice, or look away, but in Kazakhstan, they will lock eyes in a way that in many other places would be seen as provocative, almost a come-hither look. It's very pleasant—accompanied as it frequently is by a smile and a sense of recognition or greeting or even invitation—and it made it easy to meet people or to ask for a picture, to which almost everyone said yes. But it also made sense of the comment that the retired cop in Almaty had made to me, his disgust at the way women in Iran were treated, as well as of my guide to Khoja Ahmed Yasawi's mausoleum and her unflustered tolerance of my mansplainment. This is a culture in which women have real power, in which they are as unafraid as men. Perhaps this is why they could perform the mock-rape, mock-husband-beating horse chase, an unembarrassed acknowledgement of the seesaw of dominance. My guide was not about to be told how to do her job by any man, especially one as ill-informed as me—why should she?—and it wasn't just that she knew her history. She had no habit of polite deference to male opinion, no habit of even pretend deference, just a professional tolerance of foreign ignorance. That I was a published professor was interesting to her, but it did nothing to alter the basic hierarchy of knowledge—I was not anywhere near the top of it, and she knew that she was.

I kept running into perfect examples of the combination of cosmopolitan modernity and traditionalist provincialism that made the Kazakhstan I saw. The first was a man who was waiting in his car outside the mausoleum who agreed to take me the eighty miles southeast to Shymkent. He was watching a TV show on a tablet mounted to his dashboard, and when we agreed on a price and I got in, he left the show on. It played like a soap opera, and although nobody spoke English, it was easy to see that it was a popular show and produced in Kazakhstan. The actors were all, as on American TV, better looking than anyone on the street, with squarer jaws on the men, more delicate, symmetrical faces on the women, all tall and elegant, and that was true for the rich characters and the working stiffs. The action was in a mansion that was set on a large estate with stables and riding rings. In one of the rings, a man was practicing the trick riding I had watched in the Nauruz celebrations. It wasn't clear to me whether the man was being trained or the horse was, but that was secondary, anyway. The rider was mixed up in either a romantic intrigue or criminal activity or both. He insisted on completing his training session, to the consternation of two other characters anxious to either confront him or continue to co-conspire. The rider's motivation was also unclear—he may have kept riding because he was unsure what he was going to do or say next, or because he was a consummate professional who didn't let anything get in the way of his horsemanship. Or it could have just been that the producers knew how much pleasure viewers got from watching him in the ring and were eager to stretch it out as long as possible.

The driver spent a little bit of time watching the road we were driving down and quite a bit of time continuing to follow the show. I didn't feel in any particular danger—there was little traffic on the two-lane highway and it was in good shape. In the cities, the driving could be nerve-racking; watching kokpar being played, I realized that some of the driving style results from a sense that pushing people out of the way was just the way one played the game—you only get ahead by shoving your way through. And watching the little kids who excitedly risk their lives on the racetrack had something to do with it as well—a certain fearlessness was endemic. As in most places in the world, the way people drove was an expression of culture, and as in most places, the economic incentive to avoid actual crashes ameliorated the worst consequences. Of course, this may all be projection, but I kept one eye on the road, one on the screen, and hoped that while my driver watched a soap opera of a man doing death-defying horse tricks that were a thousand years old, between the two of us we had the road covered.

The driver was happy to take me, he said, because he had an errand to run in Shymkent and was glad to have a fare to get him there. Shymkent is the third most populous city in Kazakhstan, after Almaty and Nur-Sultan, just topping seven hundred thousand souls, and there are a few newer buildings, some as much as twenty stories high. But it has the feeling of an outpost—it is almost 450 miles west of Almaty, 600 miles east of the Caspian Sea, and surrounded by the grazing lands of the steppe. It feels like a small town, perhaps because half the people in the city have arrived in the last twenty years, and many of them live on the outskirts in Soviet-style apartment blocks rather than in the center, meaning that downtown, less than a square mile, hasn't changed that much—a large statue of Lenin, one outstretched hand reaching into the future, still presides over the central park. In any case, it feels moderate, contained, quiet. Which is why I was surprised when I asked my driver which of the two cities he liked better, and he shuddered at the thought that Shymkent was in the competition.

"Shymkent? No, a metropolis," he said as we drove through the countryside. "I don't like a metropolis. It is okay to go there for relax for a few days, but no, I get my comfort here, in Turkistan. I will stay here."

Turkistan has a fifth as many people as Shymkent, and the tallest buildings are a few stories shorter, but otherwise they felt comparable—neither was a village, neither felt unmanageable. Maybe my sense of things was complicated by having come from Almaty, which can't be mistaken for anything but a metropolis, and having spent my days there in an enormous Intourist-style hotel that had seen better days. The ceilings were all high enough for a state visit from Brezhnev, the paint job was from around that same era, and the staff had that Soviet disdain for the main agent of capitalism, the customer. Marx was right that the capitalist system was alienating—at least it was at that hotel. And part of that alienation was the result of having everything traditionally Kazakh stripped from the place. The brutalist building was identical to the former Intourist hotels I'd seen in Kiev and Minsk and Tbilisi and Moscow. The local had been displaced by the socialist future, tradition had been replaced with concrete.

So I agreed with my driver, let's watch the crazed horsemanship, I thought, not the road, let's stay in tiny Turkistan with its twelfth-century monastery, not big crazy Shymkent with its Oklahoma City–sized, metropolitan problems. Kazakhstan, like many of the Silk Road countries, has an interesting mix of ancient and recent history—there's a deep hospitality culture that predates Marco Polo, and people are open and cordial and helpful most of the time. But they also had, principally in Almaty, their share of Soviet-style distrust and brusqueness. Some workers had a "the customer is always a nuisance" ability to ignore you at will and other cultural holdovers from its days as Soviet Socialist Republic. But most were very kind.

At the airport in Almaty, on my way out of the country, there were three airline employees sitting at their posts, ready to check people in for the flight. I was early, and there aren't that many flights out of Almaty, so I walked straight up to the counter. The man ignored me and continued talking to his colleague at the next station. I walked over to the third station and that woman waved me away—pointing across the hall. Walking over to the other side, I flagged down an airline employee who was on her way somewhere and asked where I was supposed to go. She pointed out an older couple standing next to a small sign with the airline's name. There was a line painted on the floor in front of them and a chain across two stanchions, with the two of them in an unintentional dada performance, like two cows in a wide-open prairie standing expectantly in front of a stop sign. I asked if we weren't supposed to go to the counters, and she said, yes, but that those counters did not open for processing until 6:00. It was 5:58.

Meanwhile, a group joined the older couple, accompanied by great piles of baggage. I got behind them, watched the three people at their desks gab with each other. It was 6:05. Then 6:10. Two of them got up and went over to the coffee shop. At 6:20 they came back with coffees, the third got up and took the chain down, and the now one hundred or so people moved toward the counters and formed three restive lines.

I remembered asking an arts student in Shanghai how things had changed in China in recent years, and she said that now, with China's entry into the global economy, everyone had needed to change their work habits. For her parents it was difficult because they worked in a chemistry lab, but they were party members, so they never had to do much work. They were the kind of people, she explained, who, as an old saying went, always had a hot cup of tea in their hands. It took me a minute, but then I realized she meant they spent more time caring for their tea than for their job. These workers cared more for each other than the line of ticket-holders, and who can blame them?

These reminders of the socialist past ("Whaddya mean you can't repeat the past?" as Bob Dylan sings, "of course you can!") were offset by constant reminders of cosmopolitan modernity. As I walked across the tarmac an hour or two later, for instance, after I finally got through the line at the ticket counter, an airport worker, wearing big orange noise-canceling headphones and a reflective safety vest, walked by on some errand, singing along with Frank Sinatra, quietly, to himself and somewhat tunelessly, "I did it . . . my way . . ."

MADAGASCAR

The red clay houses, red rivers, red earth.

About sixty miles out of the capital, something was wrong with the van. The engine sputtered a bit and had little power. We pulled over, looked under the hood. The driver, Joel, pulled a case out from under his seat and hooked up his laptop computer to the van's diagnostic port. He called his boss, and they discussed it in Malagasy.

"The gas is bad," he said—we had filled up on the way out of town. "This sometimes happens," he added. "In Madagascar sometimes the gas is not good. We wait for a new car. No problem, one hour. This is Madagascar!"

"The fuel pump?" I asked.

"Yes, wet, water in the fuel."

We drove in low gear into a village, the engine sputtering a little, pulled over and went into a lunch place, had a slow lunch, and I walked around the town. In a small building with a ceiling just a few inches above my head, three young men, maybe sixteen or eighteen years old, were making aluminum pots. They packed a big pot—eighteen inches in diameter, two feet deep—with dirt and turned it upside down. They lowered a frame around it and then packed dirt around that, getting up and tamping it down with their bare feet. Outside, charcoal fires kept a few pots of aluminum molten. I could see on the ground that at least part of the aluminum had come from dead engine blocks, which had been sledge-hammered into pieces.

The very young man in charge scooped some sludge off the top of the buckets of molten lava, then went back inside to finish making the mold. He carefully lifted the frame, with its packed dirt inside, off the pot, then pulled the pot off, leaving a perfect pot-shaped, fat cylinder of dirt, and then lowered the frame back down, leaving a gap between the packed dirt top and bottom. He brought in the bucket of molten aluminum between a set of tongs, and while his assistants stood on the frame to keep it from moving, poured the liquid metal into a couple of tubes. The bare feet of his assistants were at most three or four inches from the steam. Everyone was sweating from the added heat.

Then it was over, in a matter of minutes, the aluminum had set, they pulled the frame out, knocked out the dirt, which one of the young men put through a large sieve to get it ready for the next pot, and there was the new pot, bright and silvery. They used a few rags to protect themselves from the still hot metal and pulled it off the inner dirt, which also got broken up and sieved while the boss knocked off some tabs here and there, cleaned up the handles with a rasp, and wiped it all down. Meanwhile, the other helper was filling the mold-pot with dirt again, starting on the next one. I thought of an OSHA inspector watching the molten aluminum just missing the workers' bare feet. A woman came by with her one-year-old on her hip and small metal tray. One of the boys used a pair of tongs to give her a half-dozen hot coals out of his aluminum smelter—to start a fire at her home, I assumed.

My driver's boss came with a mechanic, and we moved our stuff into their jeep and left them to deal with the van. It was an eight-hour drive to our destination, which was the next town big enough to have a small hotel, so we started as soon as they handed Joel the keys.

The roads, advertised as the worst in the world, were actually not bad, at least the main roads. Here and there, side roads were just two dirt trails through the scrub, but ours, the only through road from Antananarivo—or Tana, as it is called—to the south and the cities on the west coast, was paved and in decent shape. Cars and trucks were few and far between. Most of the traffic was on foot, bicycle, rickshaw, or horse wagon. The rickshaws were sometimes drawn by a bicycle, sometimes by a man on foot.

There were also larger, human-drawn delivery wagons, their big loads pulled and pushed down the road, often with three or four men pushing from the rear, helping the man between the shafts in front. Some were piled with thirty or more hundred-pound bags of cement, stacks of hay, produce, or metal. The grimy, seared, striving men pushing and pulling them were sometimes barefoot, sometimes in rubber thong sandals. They moved things through the center of the city and in from the countryside. Hot work, even in the mornings, the sun a scourge by 9:00 a.m., mosquitos hatching in the rice paddies, and almost no shade to be found.

We passed four men riding bicycles, each with an enormous sack of onions behind him and another on the handlebars. On the other side of the road, women were winnowing rice, whacking the sheaves against the ground, and laying out ears of corn to dry under the African sun.

Or not African. Joel was insistent that Madagascar was not Africa.

"We are Malagasy, not Africa," he said. "And in Tana, we are Merina, not Africa. Some other places in Madagascar has some Africa people, but not Tana."

"But many people come to the capital from all over the country, don't they?"

"Yes, it is a problem," he said.

"So they are not Merina."

"No, but in Tana, we are Merina. And all here—he motioned at the countryside—is Merina. Tomorrow, we will be in Sakalava people land. Also later, in Bezanozano." He shrugged. "Maybe they are some Africa," he said, "the Sakalava people. But also Malagasy."

"And you can tell by looking what ethnic group someone is from?"

"Of course," he said. "You are white! You see? I can tell right away! I am good at this!" That made us both laugh.

I could not tell the difference. I'd been all across southern Africa, with its many peoples, and could see that the people in Mozambique did not look exactly like the people in Botswana or Lesotho or Swaziland. But they all, like everybody in Madagascar, looked African to me. And if you met Joel in New York or Los Angeles or Atlanta or Des Moines, you would assume he was African American. Tana was much like Maputo or Dar es Salaam, and the countryside had the vegetation of Malawi but was flatter. None of those places were very far in air miles.

But—no surprise—Joel was right about the Malagasy. Linguistically, they are Austronesian, closer to Pacific and Southeast Asian languages than African. And the Merino have a rice-based agriculture too, so the food culture was more Asian than African, despite the French and Arab touches here and there. Whatever mixing had been going on for millennia, they were first Pacific and Asian, not Bantu, Zulu, or Somali.

And gradually I was able to see what he was talking about. As we drove toward Morondava, we passed from Merino land to Sakalava country, and there was a noticeable change. People had darker skin, curlier hair—they were a different tribe. And they were poorer too, the towns less modern, more naked kids, fewer businesses, the villages more ramshackle, reminding me of poor African villages in Mozambique and Malawi across the water. And the rice fields disappeared, replaced by dry land that looked like the Zimbabwean bush more than the wetland surrounding Tana.

Joel was a handsome young man. At first I thought he was in his twenties, but as I learned his story, it was clear he had to be in his thirties. He had the muscular, low-center-of-gravity body of a rugby player, or maybe I just thought that after I learned he had played professionally, had been on Madagascar's national rugby team in international competition. He wore Metallica and Def Leppard T-shirts and played bass in a heavy metal band in Tana. He had three young daughters, and he made good money when he was driving tourists, although it was sporadic and hard to rely on.

He worked mostly for one tour company but was a gun for hire, as many of his friends in the trade were, and would work for whoever called him. He was very personable, very good company on the road, and I told him I thought he would do well if he opened his own shop.

"Yes," he said. "The dream. But to buy a car here is too expensive. Many taxes. Two times price of car."

"Twice the price?"

"Yes, for twenty-thousand-dollar car we pay forty thousand."

"Can you get a loan?" I asked. I figured his boss was making it work—he had several cars with freelance drivers driving for him.

"Interest is 50 percent," he said. And when I looked shocked, he added, "Yes! Impossible!"

He outlined his personal finances—so much a year for health insurance for him and his family, so much for rent, for food, for the kids. He worked hard, and his wife worked, but it was just enough to get by, not enough to start a business.

Still, as we drove far from the capital, he had to admit that whatever his problems, it was nothing like those of the people in the countryside.

Houses are made of sticks and mud with thatched roofs. There is no electricity across most of the country, save a rare gasoline generator in one of the small villages along the road. In Ankotofosty—a village of about a thousand people, I saw a satellite dish on a house, and I said, "Ah! Electricity."

"Yes," he said. "They have generator. And maybe they charge people to come watch TV, or they sell some drinks or food, to pay for gas."

"So still no grid?"

"No, only in Tana. And some smaller cities. No grid in the countryside."

All around us, fields were on fire. "Why?" I asked. "Why the fires?"

"Crickets don't like the smoke," he said. It was agricultural pest control. "But I want to show you this."

He pulled over across from a large, ancient tree, with massive intricate roots showing for a few feet out of the ground. Hundreds of pieces of string and ribbon were attached to its branches.

"This a sacred tree," he said. "From old days."

"Sacred?"

"Yes, I don't know why, but very important tree."

We got back in the car and drove long stretches of nearly empty country, twenty or thirty miles between towns, with low scrub and only an occasional person walking or riding an old bike on the side of the road.

"Does anyone live out here?" I asked, pointing to the long horizon.

"No, only in villages."

"I keep expecting to see sheep or goats."

"No, not here. Now it is green, but then the grass dies and there is nothing for them to eat. Sheep only other places."

We drove toward the giant baobab trees on the west coast, listening to his music, a mix of pop and metal. He was excited about it, the way we are when sharing music we love to play. His bass had a twisted neck, he said, so most notes were out of tune, however he tuned it. He couldn't play until he got it fixed. He knew about the adjusting screw, but it was twisted in two ways— the screw couldn't fix it. He had taken it to a music store. They said there was nothing to do. It was an Ibanez five-string, and I said maybe he could get a replacement neck.

"In Madagascar?" he said, with a sad smile. "We don't have these things."

I told him I'd see if I could find one in the US and send it to him. He said that would be awesome. We drove along with the music for a while. It was okay, not my cup of tea, but I liked it better through his ears. He agreed that it was a niche, especially in Madagascar. Only he and his friends were real fans. Now that his bass neck was warped, there was nobody playing it in Tana. He turned it back up, playing his favorite tracks, trying to make me a convert.

"Why?" he asked at one point, turning down the music and looking at me. "Why is Madagascar poor? We have gold, we have zebu, we have rice, we have resources." It wasn't a question—just an opening for a conversation.

"Zebu?"

"You know, like steaks."

"Beef?"

"No, zebu. A lot of people blame the French."

"The French?"

Two men jogged by with big bales of rice straw on their heads. Jogged. Barefoot. With a hundred pounds on their heads. People worked hard. A woman peddled furiously at a small wooden, foot-operated threshing machine on the side of the road as a man fed it sheaves of grain.

"Yes, me personally, I don't like the French. The French still have a lot of power."

"I didn't know that," I said.

As we came across a bridge, naked kids, gleaming wet, ran across the road in front of us to jump in the river again.

"Yes, they still make all the decisions. I know the French. I was in French Foreign Legion. I was in training here and in France, and then they sent me to Afghanistan. My mother made me quit. 'I don't want you to die in Afghanistan,' she said. So I quit. But I met many people in Foreign Legion that I like, good people, from Congo, from Guiana, you know Guiana?"

"Yes."

"From Senegal. But not the French. I don't like. They are racist."

We rolled past a girl on the side of the road who dropped her sari for a second, then pulled it back up. A quick advertisement.

"Yes," Joel said. "People here are very poor. And so, why? Why do girls need to sell themselves? Why does the government get driven by the French? I have a question," he said.

He meant "that is my question." But it wasn't a question, it was an accusation.

There is a French cultural presence in Tana—a fancy foie gras restaurant, for instance, and a less fancy foie gras restaurant—but to me its Frenchness looked small, like remnants. For Joel it loomed enormous. For the rest of my time in the country, I asked people about it.

"Yes, the French ruined the country," one man told me. "All the French countries in Africa," he said, "they all have the same problems."

He was fifty years old, lived in Tana, and he worked several jobs to get by.

"Look at Mali!" he said. "Côte d'Ivoire! Djibouti! Terrible. The British colonies—South Africa, Ghana, Nigeria, Malaysia—they have some problems, but they are so modern, so rich. The French just took; the British built things. The British colonies—India! It is a world power!—the French colonies are lost to time!"

"And you think Madagascar's problems are just left over from that," I asked. "That colonialism is the source of them all?"

"No, not just colonialism. Then it was France, now it is still France—they meddle."

"Neocolonialism," I said.

"Yes! *Neo*colonialism. We cannot do anything without checking with France."

"But why?"

He smiled. "Ah!" he said. "That is *haute politique*!"

I asked him to elaborate, but couldn't get him to say more. "You mean corruption? Bribery?" He just wagged his finger, and repeated: "high *politique!*"

His first wife, he told me, ran off with a Frenchman. No, he said, he wasn't suggesting any connection—it's just that the French were not to be trusted.

"But neither was my wife!" he added, wry but matter of fact. They had had three kids together, but he got a divorce after she was gone for a year. He had two kids with his second wife. The first three kids, he doesn't know. Maybe they lived here, maybe in France.

The more we talked, the clearer it was that the French were not the only people he had trouble with. The Muslims, he said, were taking over the mining of minerals.

"They fight," he said. "They have a gun in the hand. Like Texas, like a film."

And the Chinese, he thought, were bad too.

"They don't build anything for the community," he said. "They don't hire local people. They are just in it for themselves. They take, they don't give, the Chinese. They are like the French all over again."

I have started to notice, as I travel, that some people, when they see a stranger, are immediately interested, wanting to look, to see, to discover something new, while others barely seem to notice, have no curiosity, are not moved to look at the world any differently than they had before the stranger crossed their path. And when I am driving—or, as in Madagascar, when I was being driven—this difference can be seen in fast motion. Some people see the stranger driving by, and they are captured by the image, they try to make eye contact, even wave, and follow the car as it moves away, while others never look up from the path below their feet for more than a glance. Some people, it seems, are focused only on the world they already know, and some peer with interest into the passing caravan. They want to know—what is it like elsewhere? What does it mean to be a stranger, to be this stranger? Where do these strangers come from, where are they going, how do they live, what are their lives? Some want to stay in their own world. Some want to know about others.

And you can see it in the smallest children, two of them playing together, one oblivious as the stranger passes, one intrigued. Or maybe oblivious is the wrong word, the child sees the stranger, she just does not find the fact of the stranger—or strangers in general—worth her time. But the other kid, she is intrigued. That kind of kid instantly recognizes a possibility, a portal, an opening, potential. Joel was one of those kids, one who wondered about the world they didn't know. That's why he joined the French Foreign Legion. That's why he asked questions.

And of course strangers come to town for many reasons—business, a quest, a mission, or, sometimes just because they too wonder about the world they don't yet know, the world that still seems immeasurable. They arrive in a strange land and understand that they are indeed strangers, that they must be strangers in order for everything to be strange. These are the people in the stories that begin, "A stranger came to town . . ." They are the strangers that make kids like the kid Joel was stand up and peer into the passing car and smile at this unfathomable person from far away. . . .

We met a cheerful friend of Joel's at a national park full of giant lemurs. The lemurs call riotously to each other in the trees, sounding like a cross between airhorns and a catfight, shockingly loud plaintive wails in the otherwise silent rainforest. Joel introduced the man by his Malagasy name, Tseetsix.

"Call me Jeff," he said. "My real name sounds too much like a pharmaceutical brand."

They were quite fond of each other, joking like beloved brothers, Jeff, the older brother, bragging about Joel's accomplishments—as a rugby player, as a musician, as a soldier. The year before, they had worked as combination drivers/guides/interpreters for an NGO that helped other organizations collect survey data. They had worked for the Malagasy Lutheran Church for a while as it was assessing the impact of Christian missions in the southern part of the country, one of the poorer regions, where only five percent of the people have any electricity and three-quarters of the children are malnourished. And they had worked for a delegation from the World Bank, which was trying to get information about the medical needs of people in distant villages and bring medical help while they were at it.

"Yes," Joel said. "Far village, poor people, sick people." And we were somber for a minute, feeling our privilege. The eerie lemurs screamed.

In high season in Morondava, Joel said, the Avenue of the Baobabs was crawling with tourists. This was the place where they took the picture on the cover of your guidebook to Madagascar, the picture on the banner of your article about Madagascar, the picture on the home-page of your Madagascar tourist agency. In season, he said, hundreds of 4×4s fill the parking lot and overflow down the sides of the street for a mile and more.

When we were there, only a half dozen cars were parked next to ours, one for a family from the town doing a photo shoot of their family to give to a relative as a present. The countercultural photographer, a bohemian guy with a marijuana leaf on his hat, was set up with reflectors and tripods and an assistant. The young women in the family vamped for the camera, the young boys horsing around. The oldest daughter encouraged me to take some photos of the family too.

"I think you are practicing with me," I said. "Getting ready before you do the real photos."

"Bien sur!" she said.

A young Black woman was walking by herself, and something told me she was American, which she was. She was doing a joint MD/PhD program at Harvard in neuroscience. We talked about what that meant in her case, what kind of research she wanted to do, my own forays into the neuroscientific literature, some of the big names in her field. She had come to Madagascar alone for the same reason I had—we agreed traveling solo was the best way to talk to people—and because, well, she wanted to go to Madagascar.

We gazed up at the gigantic, fat, magnificent red trees, with their goofy, comically small fringe of foliage at the top, anchored in the red earth, and agreed we were among the very, very luckiest people on earth.

In another group of tourists, I met a woman who had an endowed chair at an elite university. She asked me what I was doing, and I said I was writing odd little travel books.

"God! That's what I want to do!" she said. "I want to write something I *want* to *write*, and not another academic piece! Or really, I want to write something I would want to read!"

She had worked at a number of Ivy League schools and their equivalents, had published with the top university presses. Now she was pretty much at the pinnacle of her field.

"Nobody reads my books," she said. "And I don't blame them. I don't read *their* books. I don't even read my *closest friends'* books anymore. Don't get me wrong, I love doing my research and love writing my academic books, and I *do* see the value in the whole shebang, I do. But enough already. I'm done with all that. It was always so wrapped up in status anxiety and some sense of getting on the cutting edge of something, while of course I always knew our articles would be fish and chips paper in a year or two—except that it isn't even that useful, it's just dead weight on a shelf in a few hundred libraries! At least fish and chips paper has a real function."

She wasn't unhappy, she wasn't complaining really, in fact she was jolly, and she talked about her work the way we can talk about the stupid stuff we did as teenagers. No real regrets, nobody got hurt, just that what was fun at the time no longer was. I suggested as much.

"That's right," she said. "Except the ol' passing-of-time business! I just keep asking myself, shouldn't I be doing something else? Shouldn't I do at least one other thing before I shuffle off?"

Joel and I stopped at a music store, back in Tana, just before he dropped me back at my hotel. We talked to the men there about fixing his bass neck. They said it couldn't be fixed, it needed a new neck, but they had no way to get one. They had tried. We jammed a little, each taking turns on the drum set, the bass, a keyboard, a guitar. We were all about the same, except an older guy who could really play the piano, and a very young guy who was a bass virtuoso—once he played, Joel waved off offers for him to get back on it.

As he dropped me off, I asked him a question I had asked him each place we had stopped over the last ten days—we were back in Tana now, the middle of the city—is it safe to walk at night here?

"Yes," he said, "it's fine, I don't worry." But then he caught himself. "Oh, no, for you? At night? No—it wouldn't be safe. Not enough lights. And racism."

"Racism? Because I'm white?"

"Yes," he said, like *duh*.

"Because they will think I'm French?"

"No, well maybe, but just white."

I asked my taxi driver on the way to the airport: what do you think is the future for Madagascar? He repeated my question, and smiled for his one and only time that ride.

"We need hospitals. The government has to stop charcoal production. We lost 70 percent of our forests since 1980. Seventy percent!"

"Do you think they can do that?"

"We need schools." He thought. "'You can't eat roads,' our president says, but he does nothing. Nothing."

We were driving along the airport road, a stretch I'd been on several times, with its endless stream of foot traffic, bicycles, rickshaws, livestock, rice fields on either side, laundry drying on the levee walls.

"But you should tell people," he added, as if remembering what he had wanted to say all along. "Madagascar is good. Madagascar is good for tourists."

"You get a lot of tourists already, don't you?" I asked. "I mean, maybe not right now, in the off-season, but the rest of the year?"

"Not like before, not enough anymore. We get too much bad press. Especially we get too much bad press from the French. Tell people, Madagascar is good."

I couldn't find an Ibanez bass neck, not one that fit his model—everyone in Madagascar used the five-string model, but they were rarer in the US. I looked at a few on eBay that he might use for parts but ended up just getting a new one and sending it his way. When it arrived he went to the airport to pick it up and sent a picture of it strapped to his motorbike for the ride home. Heavy metal would continue in Madagascar.

HONG KONG & MACAO

The television in my Hong Kong hotel room on November 8, 2016, was showing street footage from the night before. Riot police had set upon some fifteen thousand demonstrators, swinging batons, spraying pepper spray from industrial-size canisters, and releasing tear gas. In recent days, two prodemocracy representatives who had just been elected to the Hong Kong legislature were unseated by the government in Beijing. Widely seen as part of the People's Republic of China's continued curtailment and containment of democracy, this reversal of Hong Kong's political will had brought people out en masse, in the largest numbers since the 2014 Umbrella Revolution. The protests were the culmination of a series of events—perhaps most egregious, the high-profile kidnapping of two bookstore owners a year earlier—that people saw as the PRC's deliberate undermining of freedom of assembly, freedom of speech, and Hong Kong's tradition of democratic governance, all of which were under existential threat, all essential to Hong Kong's sense of itself. This latest move was the worst so far—it attacked the democratic process itself.

And across the ocean, that same night, Donald Trump was announcing his victory in the American elections. In the US, many were talking about the death of democracy and the collapse of civic discourse that Trump's ascendancy signaled, but in Hong Kong, that felt wildly hyperbolic. The next day, I went to a studio for a radio show with Alec Ash, a writer and journalist and the editor of the *Los Angeles Review of Books*'s magazine, *China Channel*. I was in a mild state of shock, having never thought Trump would win and feeling that it was a dreadful day for America. Alec, a Brit, said that *he* was surprised that all his American friends seemed, like me, to be so surprised.

"Isn't that how you do it in America?" he asked. "Eight years with one party and then the next eight years with the other party, and you just go back and forth, right? This is your normal politics."

And of course he is right—a couple of one-termers in there, but otherwise for three-quarters of a century, from Truman on, this is the way it has gone, from Republican to Democrat and back. I also found myself thinking that this is the way life looks when you are at the end of empire—Alec must know this, having grown up in England—all of a sudden, other places look more advanced, and it is undeniable that Hong Kong and many other Asian capitals look like the future. The buildings in Hong Kong all stretch to the sky, skinnier than you would expect—not wide or deep but very tall, vertiginous—more of them than you would expect, shinier than you would expect. In some neighborhoods, on the ground, the changes seem less extreme—old dim sum places with heavy plastic sheet doors and beat-up furniture, hectic waiters, diners with heads bent over their bowls, six and eight strangers at a round table, no different from twenty years ago or forty. Still, walking into the Hong Kong Metro, down one of the many escalators or highway-sized staircases, makes the average New York subway station look like something that should be in the Smithsonian.

The only place I had ever seen anything like the Hong Kong Metro was in the movies, in those near-future films that distend the reality we know into frightening exaggerations, uncanny images that manage to be both familiar and incomprehensible. It isn't just the gleaming, spotless steel and tile and plexiglass, preternaturally clean and new, it's the scale, the mass, the size, as if the world has irrevocably changed, hyperdriven into unthinkable immensity and density. My first time in Central Station, I looked down the line of commuters, calmly queued up by the thousands, and then farther down the track at hundreds of other lines, and wondered, for a minute, whether there were enormous mirrors refracting and multiplying the scene, but no, the platform did stretch toward infinity, with countless commuters, and the train that was pulling up was preposterously long.

Does this vast modernity work to promote democratic process, or does it serve to negate it? People tend to be orderly—hundreds of thousands of Manhattanites manage to pass in opposite directions on the streets because they pretty much follow the norms. But there is something uncanny about seeing so many Hong Kongers obediently lining up and waiting, patiently, for the massive stream of people exiting the trains, then calmly moving in—here we all are, with fictions of autonomy in our heads, and yet in Hong Kong we feel the opposite truth, that like cows we follow each other's tails without much thought, we are mechanically lifted along by escalators and moving sidewalks, artificial intelligence monitors our movements and opens and closes the doors of the subway and drives the trains at the perfect speed to their perfect stops, and the restaurant at the top of the stairs can predict how many of us will order beef, how many chicken, how many tofu to within a couple percentage points. We pretend we are making choices about what we are going to do when the subway engineers and kitchen staff have known for months what we were going to be doing right at that moment in that station and that street. So how can we all possibly have significant political differences? The lucky majority all work at the same sorts of jobs—sure, some are in offices, some in factories, some on building sites, and sure, people do fewer hours a week in France than in China, but we all are subject to the same capital flows and predictable downturns and spurts of "growth." We all choose the same brands, the ones that machines and algorithms direct our attention to, we all laugh at the same TV shows, we all cry at others. Would we vote to abolish this moment and throw in with another? Apparently not. The most we will do is elect some disrupters like Trump and Boris Johnson and Jair Bolsonaro and let them mess with the algorithm before we boot them and return to "normalcy."

For years in the US, radicals both left and right have been saying there is no difference between the two parties that have been trading off the White House like a relay team for the last seventy years, and yet, and yet . . . As we watch democracy threatened, we may also be beset by larger, nihilistic fears. Should we, people ask themselves in Hong Kong, in person and in the media, should we hang on to the neoliberal quasi-democratic present or submit to the totalitarian future? It may not be the choice anyone wants, but maybe all of us will need to make it someday, and maybe we already have as we aimlessly shop, following our previously scheduled programming, and wait as the data of our decisions is scraped and fed back to us. When I was there in 2016, Hong Kongers were willing to get pepper-sprayed and tear-gassed and arrested to be able to make that decision themselves rather than have it made for them.

As is to be expected in a financial capital, Hong Kong abounds in signs of wealth: lustrous high rises with gloved doormen, sprawling luxury brand stores, apartments in the sky that sell for a half billion US dollars and more, spotless luxury automobiles with chauffeurs gliding through the city, restaurant tabs of five hundred dollars per person and up. Crazy rich, you might say. Then, still wealthy but less conspicuously, there are the bohemian neighborhoods for the children of the rich and the expat bankers and traders. Further down the ladder are the endless apartment complexes, ringing the city, filled with middle-class families.

But almost a quarter of the population lives in poverty. The run-down neighborhoods have lost everything, down to the paint on their signs, and are full of old people whose children have left them behind. Almost three percent of the women in Hong Kong work as prostitutes, most of them between twenty and forty. The income disparity is not as noticeable at the busy intersections of the business districts, in the hipster neighborhoods like Soho, or on the quiet streets of the suburban neighborhoods. But it is inescapable in Sham Shui Po and other poor neighborhoods. Some of the students I met lived in crowded small apartments in the giant complexes, just as tall, on the north side of the city, all of them, they said, densely populated with extended families or subdivided among several families.

The city is second only to New York in the number of billionaires (NY 105, HK 87), while more than 20 percent of its residents live below the official poverty line, and more than 30 percent of people sixty-five or older. Many people flee to the mainland to survive.

The next day, I was at one of the larger universities, and as I crossed the campus, a young Chinese man came by me wearing a *Make America Great Again* hat. I did a double take as he walked by and he clocked it, threw up his hands, and said, "It's ironic!"

A short ferry ride away is Macao, the Las Vegas of Asia, which, like Las Vegas, is dominated by oversized casinos on oversized lots accessed by oversized roads. Both towns exist on an antihuman scale. One chandelier in the lobby of a casino in Macao is the size of my house. The rooms, the anterooms, the number of machines, the glitzy grandeur would all make Rabelais blush at their monstrous excess.

And as with Las Vegas, one needs to wander away—in motor vehicles because nothing is walkable from the money pits—to return to a human-sized environment. In Las Vegas that means neighborhoods far from the strip, and in Macao it means the few streets of the old Portuguese city.

Anthony Bourdain touched down here, so the scarce restaurants that serve traditional food are well known, but that doesn't mean they have become any more upscale or any more crowded. None have sprouted table-cloths or waiting lists, most still have Formica-topped tables and a bit of rust here and there. At mine, a woman at the next table told me she was a regular and had been for almost thirty years. When she was in her early six-ties she had moved from Portugal to Macao because she wanted a change; she was tired of Lisbon and despaired of making a life in the country. Now, in her nineties, with her hair done in a heavily sprayed bouffant, her skirt suit not new but not overly worn, her stockings heavy, her pearls in place, and her makeup careful, she was enjoy-ing her lunch with a bottle of wine as she did most days. She was happy with her decision to expatriate and never had reason to visit the casinos or otherwise wan-der far from the dozen square blocks around her apart-ment. Once in a while, she took the ferry to Hong Kong, and each time she was reminded she had made the right choice. She didn't like the hustle and bustle, didn't need the latest anything, and the latest everything, she thought, was what Hong Kong and Lisbon specialized in.

She recommended the fish, and I took her recommen-dation for wine as well, although I was sure I wasn't up for the full bottle she managed each lunchtime. By the time we were done, though—I heard about her son, her grandchildren, her friends in the neighborhood, most of whom were also Portuguese—I had had a few glasses. The owner stopped by and said hello, and we all had an affable hour and a half together. Having no other Por-tuguese friends, and now a bit wine sodden in the mid-dle of the day, I was left with little to do after visiting the fifteenth-century A-Ma Temple and the ruins of the seventeenth-century St. Paul's cathedral than wander back to the posthuman hotel above the ringing bells and cigarette smoke of an airport-sized casino and sleep it off. I couldn't bear going back downstairs until it was time to catch my bus to the ferry. Was this voyage worth it? I wondered, and yes, I decided, it was just a lost thirty hours or so, and I had had my lunch with a grand Portuguese lady—she would have preferred lady to woman—and so yes, I had to say, yes, it was.

TAJIKISTAN

Two close-cropped, boy-skinned Americans with southern accents were at the baggage claim with me.

"You guys military?" I asked.

"Yes, sir."

"Where are you stationed?"

"Here. Dushanbe," said one.

"At the embassy," said the other.

Was this their first deployment to an embassy? "Yes, sir," they said.

"Have you ever been in this part of the world before?"

"No, sir," said the brown-haired, bespectacled one, carrying a box of newly purchased tan boots, still in their box, under one arm. It was their first deployment anywhere, they said, after training. They had never been out of the US before. They were from Kansas and Louisiana.

The Kansas one, short and blond, smiled coyly and corrected himself: "I was to Canada once."

Tomorrow would be their first day. I asked if they were nervous.

"No, sir," the boy from Louisiana with the boots said. "They told us we didn't need to be nervous, just alert, sir."

The musical instrument museum was in a man's house—it took up the front two rooms—in a nondescript neighborhood in Dushanbe. The man, the curator, was the founder of the museum and was a musician himself. He was in his fifties, hadn't had a haircut in some time, and demonstrated a bohemian disregard for fashion. He covered his head with what looked more like a 1950s beatnik cap than a traditional or contemporary hat, and he was short and earnest and simpatico.

He gave me a tour and explained who I was seeing in the photos. One man was the most important, posing in a number of shots with other famous people, talked about in framed newspaper articles, and appearing in film posters.

"He was very popular in Tajikistan," the founder said, "and outside too. He played at Kremlin for Stalin."

He pointed to one of the movie posters.

"Also, he was famous actor in many Tajikistan movies."

He had also led Tajikistan's folk music revival in the 1930s. "He was most important man," the founder said, "to make sweet, sweet Tajik music language."

In the second room there were musical instruments, some a hundred or more years old, some Tajik instruments, some from nearby—Uzbekistan, China—some Persian, and some Western, like a saxophone, an accordion, and a piano. The local and Persian instruments were museum quality, many of them quite exquisite, and in perfect condition. The Western instruments were beat up, the piano sorely in need of tuning.

I asked if he played, and he said yes.

"I am not historic," he said. "Just musician, small musician."

I told him I was a musician as well, also small and not

historic, and he asked me to play. I sat down and did a few things on the piano—blues, R&B.

He was very complimentary, and I asked him to play. He said I should please wait—his band was coming over, they were rehearsing for a wedding they were playing that night.

We talked scales for a while, and he explained that it was the flatted second that gave the music its particular feel, especially with a suspended fourth added in. He noodled around on the piano to demonstrate. I tried it and loved the flavor immediately.

"You should play with us tonight! At the wedding!" he said.

"Oh, wow, I'm not sure if I have the chops," I said.

"No, no, no, you are great player, you should play with us!"

Two young men appeared, and the three of them sat and played a number of pieces. One played a large drum held between his knees, and the other a number of other percussion instruments, and the founder played a lute and sang lead, the others singing chorus harmonies. They had a great feel, and they were attentive to each other, very focused. It was beautiful.

They were set up in the instrument room, their normal rehearsal space, but then the founder said, come, let's play together, and they moved into the other room, where the piano was. The founder talked me through one of the tunes, and I joined in as best I could. He looked at me encouragingly. When I thought maybe I was getting the hang of it, I tried to be more active, add more. The song ended and I could tell nobody was thrilled.

"Let's try another," the founder said, and named a tune. The percussionists agreed it was a good choice, and I got the basic structure. We tried it, and at the end of that one, everyone was reassuring and said *great job! Superb!* The wedding gig was never mentioned again. I clearly was not catching the sweet, sweet Tajik groove.

The country is utterly different from its neighbors, Uzbekistan, Kyrgyzstan, Kazakhstan, and Uyghur Western China. It is Persian, for one thing, rather than Mongol/Turkic like the rest, and it feels like being west of Almaty or Tashkent, toward Iran, rather than east. You get the sense of the invading armies going back and forth, and it made me think of al-Farabi and Ibn Khaldun, the medieval Islamic political philosophers who recast Aristotle and Plato to fit their political ideas to Central Asia and North Africa. The Greeks had died out as influences in Europe but had remained important to the intellectual world that emanated from Baghdad and stretched across the Mahgreb in North Africa in the west and here in the east, and it was only centuries later that Greek philosophy made its way back into Europe, through Islamic Spain. Al-Farabi and Ibn Khaldun were both interested in conquest and replacement, and it's hard not to think of the Persians as one wave of conquerors taking over the area, just as they were beaten back by the next wave, many years later, leaving behind the people of Tajikistan. And hence the Persian lilt to the music, which I could hear but could not quite make my fingers produce.

Not far from the square was a shashlik restaurant that became my default eatery while I was in Dushanbe. The women who served there were almost all substantial—

large muscular women between the ages of forty and sixty. The women in Tajikistan wear a lot of gold and sometimes silver clothing—not just as trim, but whole cloth. These women did not. They wore full headscarves and aprons, had significant eyebrows, and walked with the steady air of those who take life as it comes, unworried because they are in control—in control of themselves, in control of their husbands and children, in control of their customers. Nobody gave these women any shit whatsoever. They found it amusing that I wanted to take their pictures, and they each kibitzed on the shots, demanding as many as a dozen reshoots until they were happy. They all had some gold on their teeth.

They fed me one meal, lunch or dinner, just about every day that I was in town, and I imagined their home lives and watched the camaraderie of their workdays. Their differences, the different roles each played in their group—the joker, the adjudicator, the philosopher, the complainer—started to emerge for me, and what they shared became more evident at the same time. They were stalwart. They stood tall. They worked hard. They never hurried. They saw everything, straight ahead and peripherally, both with their eyes and emotionally. Every day, at least one of them would say, "Take me to America!" with a big smile. I always promised I would. They liked that and gave me a friendly slap on the back as they went by.

A short young man in a presentable suit and tie fell in step with me as I walked through town and said he wanted to practice his English. He was just out of college, had a businessman's neat hairdo held with some gel, and the efficient air of middle management. He would like a job in the foreign affairs ministry, he said, so it was important that his English be perfect. He showed me his notebook, which he carried in his hand or jacket pocket at all times. In it he wrote down any English word he heard, and sometimes wrote it out a hundred times. One was "cruel, cruel, cruel, cruel, cruel . . ." across a dozen lines. His dream was to visit America. He had applied for a visa once, but his papers were rejected.

He thought that the president of Tajikistan was a wonderful man, always thinking about what was best for the country, especially what was best for the economy. Since he himself studied business, he appreciated that. No, he did not have an MBA. He had completed his undergraduate studies and was working at a bank and starting a graduate program in international relations.

He loved America and loved American music, naming Michael Jackson. He liked American film, but he had trouble naming one and didn't recognize the names Tom Hanks or Cameron Diaz or Tom Cruise.

"I like the actor," he said, "whose movies are in the ring."

"The ring?"

He mimed boxing.

"Oh," I said. "Sylvester Stallone?"

He processed, then smiled. "Yes! Sylvester S . . . St . . . Rocky! Please let me show you the city and I will describe in English, and so we are win-win."

"Where did you hear that? Win-win?"

"Television," he said, tapping his notebook—it was in there, maybe a hundred times in a row. "Here is the city gardens, main gardens."

I had walked through this park in the governmental center of the city the day before. It had an enormous statue of Samani, emir of the Samanid Empire from the late ninth to the early tenth centuries, on one end and a large statue of Rudaki, the father of classical Persian poetry from the same era, in the middle. The Samani statue said SAMANI in foot-high letters chiseled into the stone, and the other had RUDAKI chiseled in the pedestal.

"This is a statue of Samani," the young man said. I waited for him to say more, but he didn't. We walked further and he pointed to the Rudaki statue and said, "This is a statue of Rudaki."

I waited, then said, "The poet."

"Yes, the poet."

A policeman stopped us and asked me for my list. I turned to ask my new friend what "list" the policeman wanted, but he had wandered away. He was close but did not want to get caught with me, didn't want to have anything to do with the police. Hmm.

"List," the cop said, holding out his hand.

I wasn't sure whether it was a shakedown, or if I was supposed to have gotten some kind of list or kept a list of something. We went back and forth a few times, me playing the numbskull tourist with a great shrugging of shoulders and upturned palms. Acting hapless was often helpful with the police, and I was, in fact, hapless in this case—I had no idea what he wanted from me. I produced my passport with its visa page, which he looked at, but more for the idle curiosity of flipping through its pages. What worked was showing him the last hundred photos I had taken, just in the two-inch window on the back of the camera. He got bored and waved me on.

My friend joined me again and reiterated his desire to go to America.

"I need a sponsor, and I think, because you are famous person in America—"

"No, I'm not famous, how did you get that idea?"

"You write books, you are a professor at famous University of California."

"Ah . . . no, I am not famous. Sylvester Stallone is famous. I am not even famous as a writer or a professor, no."

"I think you can help me. I hope."

"I'm happy to write a letter saying we met and discussed this, yes."

"You make me very happy. Always this is my wish to see America, to see American business, see Washington, DC."

One day at the shashlik place, I saw the only other European-looking person I had noticed. He was an American, and his wife was from Kazakhstan, from Almaty.

"Yes, I met her and married her up," the man said, and she smiled.

They taught at international schools. They had taught in Almaty, where they met, at one in Uzbekistan, which they loved, now at one in Dushanbe, and next year they were going to teach in Saudi Arabia.

"Ah!" I said to the wife. "This is good because they love women there!"

She laughed. "That's not what I hear," she said.

"Are you going to wear the chador?"

"Of course," she said. "When I go in public, I will have to. But for one year I can do anything."

"The money is really good," the husband said, and she nodded agreement.

"This is what convinced us," she said.

He added, "I think it will be fun."

"Fun?" I asked. "It doesn't sound like fun to me."

"Yes," he said. "These are very strange places. I worked

in Kuwait for three years, and I would end up in a big tent in the desert, where everyone was drinking—against the law—and there was a pet tiger. Bengal tiger."

"Really?"

"Yes, a baby tiger. But other times I saw a pet cheetah, even a pet polar bear. That one pissed me off," the man said. "A polar bear in the desert!"

"And after Saudi, where will you go next?"

"Well, that's the big question, isn't it. We have to decide to come back to Almaty, or . . ."

He looked over at his wife, who looked uncomfortable. I guessed she wanted to be in Almaty, what with her family there.

"Or continue to wander?" I asked.

"Yes, continue to wander," he said carefully, glancing at his wife.

She was noticeably silent.

At the airport I checked my email. I had several new notes from the young man who showed me the gardens, the Sylvester Stallone fan. I wondered: Could I, in good conscience, write in support of him coming to the US? What did I know about him, really? Was it possible that he had been playing me? I didn't like that I was wondering this, but I was.

I never did see the American embassy, and I thought of this young man getting checked through security there by the two boys from Kansas and Louisiana as he tried again to get a tourist visa so he could see Washington, DC. They were approximately the same age. The Tajik was the more worldly of the three, better educated, and doubtless the most constrained. The Persian Empire was a long, long time ago. The statues in his city park represent Persian men who lived five hundred years before Columbus sailed the ocean blue, and even if I wrote a letter of support—and I had a quick flash of being interrogated by the FBI about why I had no suspicions of this young man, who had approached me in the middle of the city for no reason, who befriended me for no reason, who was so interested in Washington, DC, who avoided the police, and who I vouched for after knowing him for only an hour—it was a long shot that my young Tajik friend would ever discover America, while Kansas and Louisiana and California could waltz into his town whenever we wanted. The American empire was not over quite yet.

BRAZIL

I n the state of Minais Gerais, a hundred miles or so
north of São Paulo, roads head into hills full of resort
hotels. Like the Catskills or the Poconos on the East
Coast in the US, these hillside resorts cater to families from the city looking to get away for the week-
end or a week.

We flew into São Paulo from Los Angeles, a twelve-
hour flight, so I looked for a hotel just a couple hours
north of the airport and picked one in the very odd town
of Campos da Jordão. All the resorts in this town and
the surrounding hills are done in a faux Tudor style, and
many of them are enormous, as if they had been built
to film *The Magic Mountain*. At 5,500 feet above sea
level, Campos da Jordão is the highest town in Brazil,
so the Swiss theme makes a little bit of sense, but it is
carried out with a Disneyland intensity that is discon-
certing. Since we were there off-season, many things
were closed, including the restaurant in our hotel, which
gave the place a creepy feel, like *The Shining*. We went
to the only restaurant we could find, also Swiss-themed,
and I'm sure we would have become accustomed to this
with time, but we had arrived in Brazil just a few hours
earlier, so the last thing we thought we would be doing
was going to a fondue restaurant. Yes, cheese fondue.
And for dessert, chocolate fondue. We wanted to ask

how this had happened—was there some "Boys from Brazil" connection, or a Swiss émigré community? But we couldn't really ask. Nobody spoke English.

The next ring of hills north, much less populated, includes the beautiful Ibitipoca State Park, just south and west of Belo Horizante. On the edge of the park is a stone village, somewhat overrun with tourist services, called Conceição do Ibitipoca, on the edge of which is an ecoresort called Reserva do Ibitipoca.

The Reserva is the project of an heir to a copper fortune—a fortune large enough that his thirteenth of it (he has many siblings) provides him his own nature preserve and his own plane. Ernesto—I'll call him Ernesto—is dedicated to preserving as much of the natural environment in the area as possible. The park is 3,680 acres, and his holdings next to the park are now much larger than the park itself. He has placed the land in a trust, with strict preservationist restrictions. His idea is to repatriate some of the species that have been lost to development, to reinvigorate the small villages in the hills, to promote sustainable agriculture in spots, and to conduct ecological research. The Reserva is a place for high-end tourists to come and get educated on the natural environment while helping to support the venture.

The owner has the relaxed air of a man with no worries whatsoever, but he does, in fact, worry about global and local environmental degradation. On a personal level, though, he seems quite comfortable with who he is and the choices he has made. When we met, some of his kids from earlier relationships were about, as was his new girlfriend, a number of friends, and a larger number of employees—the director of his foundation, research scientists on his payroll, hotel and kitchen staff, road builders and drivers and administrators and gardeners. All appeared to be living in easy harmony, and the staff that I talked to were excited about the opportunity they'd been given to be part of the project. For people from the local area, this employment is an unexpected boon. For the environmentalists, it is a dream come true. A bit of happy idealism floats in the breeze.

It was hard not wonder what impact it would have on his personality if Ernesto didn't look like a Brazilian George Clooney—ageless salt-and-pepper, Hollywood jawline, long eyelashes, movie star charisma, and a metabolism that shaved a good decade off whatever his age was (which one guesses based on the age of his adult children). He wears this all lightly and is unaffected when he talks, happy to share credit with everyone, happy to insist that he is just one of the cogs in the machine they are running together.

He has the disposable income to match his vast ambitions, and he continues to gobble up all contiguous land the minute it becomes available, including, recently, an entire mountain village. The conservationist project and research is admirable and is directed by respected botanists and other scientists. Even the beautifully detailed nineteenth-century fazenda with ten-foot ceilings built for use as the hotel can be justified as an act of historical reconstruction, and it is so beautifully done and artfully distressed that it was like being in a museum. But then there was the kitchen: the pony-tailed young man who was introducing us to the Reserva asked if we recognized it, with a glint in his eye, and we said no; it turns out that, in response to a request from the owner's son, the kitchen was built as a faithful replica of the kitchen in *Ratatouille*, with green enamel ovens and copper everywhere, which was, well, beautiful and conspicuously extravagant—in and of itself and especially as the result of the whim of an eight-year-old.

But as I write this I think—what is this, envy? Much as I like to think envy is an emotion I'm largely free of, since after all, lord knows I have had more than my share of good fortune, I have to assume there's some. Why else is George Clooney showing up here? And what's with the "kids from earlier relationships" and "new girlfriend"— since when am I such a judgmental prude?

That night we were to join the man and his friends at the new village. He said the driver would pick us up at 7:00 to be his guests at his new vegan restaurant. I said I was happy to drive, but he said, no, no it would be much better if Mario took us in the four-wheel-drive jeep, as he knew the road and it was tricky—*new road*, he said, with a smile that said trust me, I know better.

Devoted to the Reserva and to his boss, Mario was a sympathetic and smart young man, with an infectious, puppyish energy. He had grown up on a farm in the mountains, as had his father before him and his father's father. I asked what had changed since the project started, and he pointed to himself as a prime example.

"I never would have gone to college," he said.

"Did your boss make that possible?"

"Yes, he paid for everything, paid a helper for my father on the farm too. He wanted me to study biology so I could help with the experiments."

"That was his idea?"

"Yes, but it was my idea too. I already helped with the fish beds and the planting. I wanted this, to study biology."

"Do you think you would have stayed in the hills if Ernesto had never bought the Reserva, or would you have gone to the city?" He was smart and ambitious, and smart ambitious kids typically do head down to Rio or São Paulo.

"I would have stayed and worked on the farm, just like my father. I never thought of doing anything else—I loved the farm because I love biology! I didn't know it was biology! Ernesto changed everyone's life here."

"Did he send everyone to college?"

"No, this is not for everyone. But for everyone, the world changed here. The world came *here*."

He had first taken a part-time job on the grounds crew. And he was happy with that job, would have been okay with that, he said, it was a good life, better than most people in the mountains could hope for, but, well, "everything changed."

"What do you mean, everything?"

"I wouldn't be speaking English to you, for one thing," he laughed. "I learned at college, and Ernesto made that happen. I am grateful. The scientists who come from all over the world, they speak English. They help us think about our different projects. But all these people, our neighbors, everyone lives better now. Almost everyone."

We took the jeep across a field, and as the sun set we followed the freshly cut road into the forested mountains. A half hour in, Mario stopped beside a large pond in the dusk and turned off the engine. We stepped out of the jeep. Frogs chirped, the pond black and still, the sky cobalt, just enough light to see everything in outline, dark enough to bathe the scene in mystery. Some wisps of fog had started to form a foot above the pond. Mario may have been on the research team, but he was evidently on the hospitality team too and knew this was a beguiling spot, knew he was giving us the full feel of the place.

We drove into the dark wood, the fresh-cut road angry, wet, and red, as if bleeding, loose and unstable, the jeep leaning downhill the whole trip. Rain had pooled here and there, and the four wheels spun now and then, making me glad, on the one hand, that I hadn't tried to drive it myself, and on the other, thinking that Mario might go slower, that slower might be more relaxing. Before this new road, it took several hours, he said, to drive down the valley and back up the next one to get there, and now it was just forty minutes or so. But most of those forty minutes were terrifying. I had faith that this kid at the wheel knew what he was doing, but he was young, and the jeep was sliding, the drop-off steep into the dark.

On the far side of the ravine, we came to a small village with stone buildings and a few saddled horses parked alongside a scattering of cars. It was tiny even compared to tiny Conceição do Ibitipoca and had no visible relation to the tourist trade. Conceição had dozens of little tourist shops, this village none. That makes sense, since Conceição is at the gate to the National Park, and this small village is off every beaten path. The vegan restaurant that Ernesto hadn't quite opened to the public had no sign. But the staff were there, and they were preparing a meal for us and for some other people staying at the Reserva, for Ernesto and his friends, and a few locals.

Before dinner we got a concert of traditional music in a small amphitheater (which Ernesto had also just built), played by a musical troupe of a half dozen young people, crunchy types, the men with long hair and buns and beards, the women in hippie skirts, some dreadlocks here and there, beads. They were playing through amplifiers and a portable PA system, but there were no lights, so the band became increasingly difficult to see as the night deepened. They were from the city but earnest and learned in the country music tradition that none of them had grown up with. That music, the leader told me through an interpreter, was important to conserve, just like the land. They were competent and disciplined players, if unexciting, and some of the local people came to watch. Eventually, we all started to dance, standing around the amphitheater, as the drum-based music went from tune to tune, each with a close family resemblance to the tune before, all sorts of protosamba but with less African influence—folksongs representing the way cultures had mixed a hundred years earlier.

After the concert we went into the restaurant and sat at communal tables in a low-ceilinged room that had been the living room of a small house. Ernesto said he liked that it was a small room.

"We have a saying here," he said. "The smaller the house, the more cozy the people."

I was sitting next to a woman who was there with her daughter and slightly younger son. The daughter went to college in the States and spoke perfect English. The mother was born in India of Indian parents and had the English accent of the subcontinent. They had a place in London and a place in São Paulo, and she was here with a couple of kids at a very expensive resort. She was Brazilian, she was stylish, she was the mother of an American college kid with multiple addresses—she was the international bourgeoisie. As a result, she felt familiar, like people I've met at bookstores, on campuses, in museums around the world, as if class molded people like a PlayDoh Fun Factory, squeezing us all out into the same shape, erasing difference with money. She was sweet and easy going, her privilege just popping up here and there, flowering once in a while in the interstices, not oppressive. Another mother-daughter duo I found less pleasant—they just rubbed me the wrong way, the woman dripping with expensive jewelry, the girl home from college in Florida. She was bored, resentful that she wasn't still in Florida, couldn't be bothered to answer a question from anyone, and gave no evidence that she had a brain in her head. Having not always lived among the haute bourgeoisie, I recognized the trait the way a revolutionary would. I'd seen such people give lesser mortals the silent treatment, the silence that says *you are not important enough for me to even acknowledge your existence*. Seeing it triggers my pitchfork- and torch-bearing peasant id, but she was just a kid, after all, and I was a guest, and so I just calmed down and went with the languid flow.

The food was laid out on a central counter and on top of a woodstove to keep it warm, and we were told to help ourselves. The women making the food—they were all women—had worked with their own recipes, augmented by some of Ernesto's, and it was quite good. My sense that this was among the most quixotic culinary ideas I had ever heard of—bringing gourmet veganism to the untrammeled countryside—was diminished, although not much, by a recognition that some of it—the squash soup, the *elote*—was standard local fare. It still wasn't clear to me, though, where a clientele for a restaurant would come from. The local people who had come for the concert had all gone home, unless they worked in the kitchen, and there didn't seem to be enough people around to support even a café.

Ernesto spent most of his time relaxing with his friends and didn't seem eager to gear up his English-speaking brain again, and since people were not drinking—we'd all had a beer or a small glass of wine, but it wasn't a drinking crowd—things broke up fairly quickly, and Mario drove us back, sliding again through the red mud, lit and shadowed by the bouncing headlights, to the Reserva and its elegant rooms.

On Sunday downtown Rio de Janeiro was deserted. In December, the heat and humidity was intense, and just walking worked up a sweat.

As we passed the remnants of the old aqueduct, the Arcos da Lapa, a group of young men lounged about, and I clocked them as a possible problem. They were in their late teens and early twenties, looked a little druggy and aimless, the classic perp profile for the massively overpopulated street-crime class of the city. We had seen them as we turned a corner and so had to make a split-second decision: one, give them as wide a berth as possible, announcing that we were afraid of them, or two, keep on our path right by them as if we were fearless and almost daring them to act, or three, a middle path, keeping on a straight line but farther from them than we would have otherwise—aware, alert, wary but confident. We decided on this option, and I gave them a hard look, saying *I have my eye on you*, for what it was worth. We felt exposed and bristly.

After a while though, when it was clear they weren't coming after us, we relaxed. We stopped at the far end of the plaza, and I checked my phone to put us back on track for the museum.

Look out! L—— screamed, and I turned to see one of the young men running at me with a box cutter in his hand, pointed at my face. I yelled at L—— to get far away, and she backed up but kept screaming, and in the slowed-down interval of adrenalized danger, I thought *wow, she sounds like the kid in* The Exorcist, *really scary.* I whirled away from the approaching blade in a move that felt well-oiled, practiced, like I was Jackie Chan or a capoeira expert, throwing my forearm up to deflect his box cutter–wielding arm as I ducked under it, doing a 360-degree spin, standing back up to face him in a fight pose, yelling *FUCK THE FUCK OFF YOU FUCK!!* And between the two of us screaming at him, and him realizing that I was stronger and more agile than he thought and maybe even trained in some martial art he hadn't run across, he slinked backward away from us. He may have been grinning, but my focus was nailed on his weapon and wouldn't let go. He walked backward, and we walked backward, keeping an eye on him, out of the square.

In the year or so since, I've told this story to friends several times, and each time that I've demonstrated the spin move that I did that day, I've lost my balance like the old doofus the thief had taken me for, ending up on the ground once, always awkward and pathetic. But that day I had somehow channeled the power of a mother picking a car up off her child, the adrenalized body making its own way in the world, independent of thought or volition, turning me willy-nilly into a martial artist for two full seconds. With any luck, I will never have to do it again.

We went on and found the entrance to the Museo Judaico, the Jewish Museum. By then we were shaky with spent adrenaline and sopping wet, ridiculously grateful to be behind a metal detector in air-conditioning, looking at the extensive record of the Jewish journalism of 1920s Rio. A half dozen different publications were thriving a century ago, mostly in Portuguese, some Yiddish. All the visitors to the museum were Americans.

L—— and I were sweating profusely and shaken by the mugging a few minutes earlier—or was it mugging? I wondered. Are you mugged if you get away? Attempted mugging? Or is that not a thing? I suppose once a knife is brandished in someone's face, it is a mugging. Anyway, the A/C was on full blast, turning my sopping shirt icy. A bit stunned, I wandered the cases, looking at issues of the different magazines and newspapers. I loved the image it gave of a culture in bloom. Everyone else seemed much more interested in the candelabras and Torahs and other sacred objects, but I was hypnotized by this distant band of print culture enthusiasts, devoted to a purely local audience in their miniature cosmopolis a hundred years ago.

The subcultural journalists of yesteryear struck me as somehow related to the subculture of unemployed youths hanging in the city like carrion birds, waiting for the weak or wounded to drop out of the sky and hand over their iPhones. Maybe it was just the aftereffects of the box cutter, or that I had been wasted by the heat, but in my still-not-dry clothes, the hardy band of Jewish writers and thinkers and the hardy band of lounging muggers under the aqueducts struck me as similar—however obviously different in myriad ways—each group huddled together for warmth and mutual support, feeling their difference from the happy goyische bourgeois in their unquestioned privilege, doing their best to make a life.

That is too simplistic, of course, and comparisons are odious. But one of my senses of Brazil comes from *Manda Bala* (*Send a Bullet*), a documentary by Jason Kohn, which profiles representatives from a number of overlapping subcultures in São Paolo—a businessman who takes helicopters from his penthouse to rooftop restaurants for dinner and bulletproofs his cars, a low-level worker in a kidnapping enterprise, a plastic surgeon who does reconstructive surgery on kidnapping victims, a policeman, and a moderately corrupt politician. The kidnapper is a poor man, living in a favela, who barely manages to get by with a large family in a small apartment. He doesn't get a cut of the profits, he just gets paid as a day laborer for kidnapping the victim, holding the victim prisoner, and, when necessary, slicing off body parts to send to whoever is paying the ransom. As he says in the film, some people steal with a gun (or box cutter); some people steal with a pen, like politicians. The kidnapper believes that the rich will remain the rich, the poor will remain the poor, and the only thing a poor man can do is find a way to steal enough to live. The rich businessman agrees: there is nothing to be done about the divide between the rich and poor, he says ("it will only get worse"), except bulletproof your life—armor your car and do most of your local travel by helicopter—all the best restaurants and shops are at the top of the high-rises anyway, because there you feel protected. We all take care of ourselves and our families as best we can, given the place we find ourselves. The Jews of Rio de Janeiro in the 1920s were protecting themselves with culture, trying to stay alive, just as the boys under the aqueduct were just trying to stay alive by stealing what they needed to steal—that day they hoped it would be my phone. The kidnapper, c'est moi; the rich man, c'est moi; the thief, c'est moi; the Yiddish journalist, c'est moi.

We left the museum, walked back into the wet heat, and took a cab to our hotel.

Christmas was upon us, and we were getting ready to leave the Santa Teresa neighborhood where we had ended up—a kind of hipster Brooklyn neighborhood on a hillside above Botafogo—to head south along the coast to São Paulo. I took a load of laundry down the hill—every walk now an adventure, with my antennae quivering, expecting to be rushed with a box cutter at any moment. The steep, curving, narrow road was lined with retaining walls covered with interesting graffiti, that work tagged by less interesting graffiti, a mark of the dividing line between hipsterdom and scarcity the road represented. I found the cleaners I was looking for, and they said they could do it, and struggling through my Spanish and their Portuguese, I got that I needed to pick it by 2:00 the next day, because it was Christmas Eve and they would be leaving early. Perfecto, I said, hoping that worked in Portuguese too. It seemed to.

The next day, I braved the hill again, heading down just before 1:00 p.m. The laundry was in the middle of everyday Rio life in the unsung neighborhoods—not a great neighborhood, not a terrible neighborhood. You could see it was nowhere to be late at night, but it was a friendly, pleasant place in the day. I got there and couldn't find my cleaners right away, went up and down the street, and put the address in my phone, the GPS function less than fully accurate in Brazil. I realized that the reason I didn't find it was because it was closed, a metal garage door lowered and padlocked in front of its sign and windows, covered in many years' layers of graffiti and urban grime. I knocked, then knocked louder, hoping they were still there packing up. It was 1:15 at the latest. No response. Many of the other businesses along the strip were closed too, since it was, after all, Christmas Eve. A man made me to understand, despite having no language in common, that the owners lived in the building, so I kept banging on the metal door. The closest open establishment was a hair salon a few doors down. I walked in and asked if anyone spoke English, and one of the women in a chair, her hair freshly shampooed, said yes. I told her my predicament, that we had an Airbnb down the coast already paid for and no clothes, and she relayed it to the other women in the shop. Nobody was sure how they could help me, but I asked if maybe the owner of the salon knew her neighbor and had some way of getting in touch. This was discussed round robin, and they came to a decision to call the owner and find out. She apparently lived in her building too, because she suddenly appeared. With the help of my volunteer translator, we asked her if she had a number for the launderers. She did, and called. Meanwhile, everything else in the salon had stopped. Everyone, some just by furrowing their brows, was working on the problem of me and my laundry.

The owner talked into her phone for a while and then handed it to me.

"I am so sorry," a man said, "but the family is in the car on their way to the mountains for Christmas, and we cannot get your laundry for two days when we are back." I wasn't sure who he was, another relative, I assumed, because the man in the laundry did not have any English.

"Ah, this is a problem for me," I said. "The man in the laundry told me I could pick up until 2:00, and I was here just after 1:00."

He consulted with the others in the car and came back on. "No," he said. "They said by 12:00." And then I remembered him saying *doce*, and me thinking, 2:00, when it was clearly 12:00.

"Ah, my mistake! Of course, he said twelve. Is there anyone here who can open the door for me?"

"No," he said. "The whole family is in the car, many hours away."

I thought huh, it isn't 2:00 yet, how can they be many hours away? But in any case, there we were. I looked up, and the whole salon was hanging on my words, anxious to know what had been said.

I explained my misunderstanding. "Thank you, thank you, gracias, obrigado, I appreciate all your help," I told them, and said I would see them in a couple days. But they were in problem-solving mode, suggesting that they mail my laundry to me wherever I was going. I thanked them again, said it was not necessary, I would come back. What a group of unequivocally lovely people! What kindness! To a random dummy who didn't know two from twelve. I bowed in gratitude.

We went down the coast, halfway to São Paolo, and stayed in our Airbnb. The day after Christmas, we drove the three or four hours back to Rio and picked up our laundry, then took the highway south once more to São Paolo. I wanted to stop in the salon and thank the women there again, but when we got there it was closed for the holiday, its own metal garage door pulled down over its front windows. I left a note.

In São Paulo, Beco da Batman is an art street, with every surface muralized, a few low-rent art galleries, and people selling their wares on the street. We liked one guy's work in particular, and he told us, in heavily accented but adequate English, searching for words here and there, that they were all figures based on the Brazilian version of commedia dell'arte. The one we liked the most was a clown—a big ruffled collar, face painted white, nose painted red, polka-dot clown suit, holding an open book. He, the artist told us, was called The Professor. He is always shown holding a book and is always dressed like a clown. The painting had a smudge at the bottom—someone had picked it up with dirty hands, I assumed—and the artist quickly mixed up some matching paint on his palette, adding this and that until he got it right, and touched it up for us. We paid him for the piece, happy to have found a piece of authentic Brazilian street art that we both liked and that we'd been able to talk to the artist about. We talked about the neighborhood, about whether he could make a living this way—it was touch and go, but his girlfriend had a good job—and asked if he had grown up in the city or somewhere else in Brazil. No, he said, he was from Tbilisi, Georgia, and had moved to Brazil just three years earlier. His Portuguese, he said, still wasn't much better than his English.

São Paolo celebrates New Year's Eve by closing more than a mile of Avenida Paulista and wiring its length with stacks of speakers and jumbotron screens to show the acts on the two-story-high stage at the northwest end of the street. Two million people come and ramble up and down the avenue, many wearing all white, with the same tiaras and goofy spangled glasses and glow sticks and sparklers as in Paris or New York or a thousand other cities. People swerve through the crowd selling plastic cups of caipirinha, the national drink of cachaça and lime, at a dollar a pop, while some revelers carry their own coolers and bottles of wine and champagne, and groups of friends hang and dance together to some of the country's biggest musical groups on the stage.

It had the flavor of a neighborhood street party, with twice as many people as cram into Times Square in New York each year. There was a massive police presence, which is perhaps why it all felt so safe. A couple of pickpockets, their eyes dope-glazed, ineffectually pushed their way through the crowd now and then, but 99.9 percent of the street was chill and happy, smiling at strangers, the old people dancing, the young people dancing, the middle-aged people dancing, everyone buzzed, almost nobody very drunk, a feeling of wide camaraderie in charge, as if a truce had been called for the night between the haves and the have-nots. Tomorrow, Brazil would return to finding its destiny; tonight, the destiny was Avenida Paulista, caipirinhas, music, and fireworks.

And the next day, the country did meet its current destiny in the inauguration of President Jair Bolsonaro, a far-right populist who, like Trump, seems to relish outraging the media that covers him, with regular comments that are flat-out racist (Blacks are "animals"), sexist (he told a female legislator he wouldn't rape her because she was ugly and not his type), and homophobic ("I would be incapable of loving a homosexual son," he said. "I would prefer my son to die in an accident than show up with a mustachioed man"). Trump loves him.

For people like the gay couple that owned the B&B where we stayed on the coast, the rise of Bolsonaro was the end of an open society. And Bolsonaro, like Trump, wants to roll back the welfare state and stop trying to alleviate the worst economic inequities. Six individuals in Brazil possess as much wealth as the poorest hundred million people in the country, half of whom live in poverty. With Bolsonaro, Brazil has voted to keep the bulletproofing and helicopter businesses afloat, maintain a small class of professional kidnappers, further expand the favelas, and leave those boys lounging under the aqueduct, waiting for the next tourist to wander by.

NEPAL

I asked at the front desk of my hotel in Kathmandu where I could eat local food. I was staying just inside the tourist center—a set of winding pedestrian-only streets chockablock with souvenir shops and hamburger, pizza, and ice cream places. The young woman was dubious and said that there was no actual restaurant she could send me to, but did I want a momo place? I said of course I want a momo place—what is momo? Momo, she said, was what truck drivers stopped and ate, what anyone who wanted a quick lunch ate, the most Nepalese food there was. The best momo place, she told me, was close by, Everest Momo, and she drew me a map. It was a few blocks out of the bubble, in the flurry of actual Kathmandu.

Only in India have I seen as much traffic congestion and air pollution and roadway mayhem as in Kathmandu—the number of beat-up cars and trucks had expanded well beyond the road system, and that meant more cars abreast than there were lanes, more irate drivers battling for precedence, more exhaust, and more honking and screeching than one could imagine, especially if one imagined Kathmandu to be the fabled, wooden-temple, mountaintop aerie I had somehow conjured. I had felt the allure of the place my whole life, had concocted a village of ornate temples sheltered from modernity by a ring of snow-capped peaks. Instead, the city was an interminable gray, concrete, crazy morass of too many people with too little space or money, with a little rundown warren of temples in the middle, the air too polluted to see any mountains anywhere.

Everest Momo was on the main drag, so a certain amount of the street came in with me as I took a seat, and with every new diner. The Formica and wooden tables and squat stools were mismatched, worn, and close together. The place was hopping, tables shared at random, and people were quiet, all parties of one sitting with strangers, all men with no reason to speak to each other. Momo turned out to be small ping-pong-ball-sized dumplings, although slightly flattened and twisted as they are crimped to hold in the filling, six or eight of them served in a half ladle of milk broth on a six-inch metal plate. A small boy, maybe nine or ten, came by with a long-spouted metal pitcher and poured fresh broth on people's plates now and then if they wanted it. I asked the server for a second plate of them, the way I had noticed other diners do it, by raising a finger. He asked me if I was American when he brought me a fresh plate.

"Yes. You speak English."

"Yes, I am in school for hospitality. I learn English and Mandarin. I like to practice."

"You work here too," I said.

"Yes, this is my family's business. I help when I can. That is my mother making momo." She was rolling out dough, cutting it up. His aunt was cutting onions. His father strained the momo out of an enormous boiling vat.

"The woman at my hotel said this was the best momo in town."

"Yes," he said, "perhaps." He was proud but knew it was just a bare-bones operation. "I want to have a hotel, with a full restaurant. Then maybe we all work there. Soon I will leave for my internship. I go to a hotel in China."

"Ah, that's why Mandarin."

"Yes. Mandarin for the staff and the Chinese guests, and English for foreign guests."

"Where in China?"

"I don't know," he said. "They do not tell me yet. They have deal with different hotels to have Nepal interns. Then I learn every part of the hotel for two years."

"Do they pay you?"

"No, but I have a bed and food, so I don't need money."

He grabbed a new plate of momo from his father for another customer and came back.

"Two years! That's a good deal for the hotel—free labor."

"Yes, but good deal for me too. Practical knowledge."

"And how do you get the funds to buy your hotel, the building, the furniture, everything?"

"This I need to learn too. We study the business in school." He was undaunted.

"And are you worried about living in China, all that time?"

"No!" he said. "We all do this in my school. China is a rich country, with many good hotels, good business. This is big opportunity for me."

He signaled his little brother to get me more milk broth and left to grab a plate of momo for a new customer, aglow with his bright future.

The next morning, I meandered my way—it's about an hour's walk straightaway—to see the Pashupatinath

Temple, or parts of it, anyway. Much of it is closed to non-Hindus, and I spent time walking around the walls and along the Bagmati River. Pashupatinath is one of the most revered temples in Hinduism, and the Bagmati, like the Ganges, is considered a sacred river. Along the walls of the temple, holy men have small one-room shrines, and people go in, worship, and come out with smudges of color—sandalwood, vermilion, crimson, yellow—on their foreheads.

A holy man, wearing a loin cloth, his long gray hair in dreads, with one dead eye and the other focused somewhere near the top of my forehead, stood in front of a doorway, out of which some smoke poured, and I went into his shrine with him. A large split log was burning in the center, with three or four feet of fresh log sticking out toward the door, the front foot or so burning amid red coals. Smoke filled the air, and I worried for the man, spending all day breathing in that much soot. Altars lined the small room, brimming with a dense collage of material objects and statues and offerings, some obviously religious, some almost comically profane: soda cans, plastic toys, a few bills and coins, candles, dried flowers, swatches of cloth, small pyramids of colored powders, and incense burners, these last adding to the thickness of the air. The man spoke at me in what might have been Nepalese or Hindi or Maithili or Newari—I had no way of knowing. He was intent, deadly somber, incanting, not in the least put off his game by my inability to respond. His concave chest was brown like a smoked fish and had a few long white hairs wandering out. His dead eye was milky, the other never landing on me or, it seemed, on anything else. It struck me that his nondead eye, which I took to be unfocused in the throes of spiritual communion of some sort, was simply not working, that he was blind. After a few minutes of prayer—or at least I assumed he was saying a prayer—he felt behind his back for a tray and put it in front of me. There were coins and bills on it, and it was time for me to make my offering. I gave the equivalent of a dollar or two, and either by feel or sound, he knew I had. He set the tray down behind him, his two unseeing eyes lost in different directions. He reached to the pile of red powder and put a smudge on my forehead, said a few more words, and that was that. We were done.

Back out in the sun and less trammeled air, down a flight of stairs with monkeys scampering across the white-washed walls on either side, around a corner, down more stairs, I came out at the river. A number of holy men were set up there too, some having a blanket spread with a dozen books and implements and sacred objects, some with a less ostentatious footprint, and pilgrims stopped in for a consultation or a tune-up or a prayer. I didn't know enough about the sects and variants to know what I was looking at, but I found the matter-of-factness, the neighborliness of the interactions between the holy men and their clients homey, so much more human than the pastor in his pulpit or the priest performing for the crowd or the rabbi singing scripture. One on one, person to person, face to face. I couldn't tell if they were meeting for the first time or came by every week or every month or every day. There was comfort and respect and ease. If this was religion, my atheist bones said, so be it.

On a parapet ten feet above the river, several funeral pyres were burning or being built. For one, men were just laying down the first logs in preparation, and a few mourners were waiting. At another, the pyre had been built, split logs were stacked like a rudimentary six-foot-square log cabin, with kindling inside, and about three feet off the ground, in the middle of the logs, I could see the body, laid out on a plank, swaddled head to toe in a bright yellow bolt of cloth, underneath further layers of logs. It was clear from the shape which was the head and which the feet. It was real, quotidian, bleak. Fifty or so mourners had gathered, most in everyday dress, looking like they might be on their working-class or shopkeeper lunch hour. Each of the cremations had started at different times, so watching the five altars from across the river, I got a time-lapsed view of the process. After the pyre is built by a crew of two, the mourners gather, the fire is set, the crew fans the flames and manages the fire as the pyre collapses, keeps everything burning down to coals, rakes them to keep them going, and then, after all has returned to dust, a man in the river scoops up five-gallon white plastic buckets of water and hands them up to the crew, who use them to wash the ashes off the altar and into the river, the coals and stone floor sizzling and steaming, until the altar is clean and ready for the next pyre to be built.

It's a tough performance to watch for an American, anyone for whom TV and film violence and death are a steady diet but for whom personal death is more hidden and private than pornography. As historians have noted, in the nineteenth century in America, death was everywhere and talked about openly—Emmeline Grangerford in *Huckleberry Finn* is the famous example, writing funeral odes for people she has never met—while talk about sex was verboten. In the twentieth century, talk about sex was everywhere, and death was not discussed in polite company. In my family, we didn't talk about death, and at funerals the caskets were always closed. I had never seen a dead human body that wasn't enclosed by a casket until that day, on the banks of the Bagmati, watching as one after another went up in smoke in the presence of their loved ones.

The matter-of-factness of the crew at work, the finality of the ceremony—the sluicing of ash into the river, everything, at the end, gone—felt both more fitting and less satisfactory than my own culture's compromise. We fetishize our ashes, but by the time these ashes were washed into the Bagmati, most of the mourners had already left. We Americans leave the crematorium with our urn full of ashes, like a miniaturization of the process by which a casket finds its earth; we come in with a body and leave with it transformed, taking the urn and parking it on a mantelpiece or shelf or ceremonially scattering the ashes in the sea or the mountains or a sacred place. But here in Nepal, the body is truly gone, its traces swirling down to the delta or out to sea, and the mourners disperse doubly bereft, with nothing. The sins of the world and the rest of it are washed away, and the mourners leave empty handed.

As I headed back up toward the temple entrance, I saw my holy man from earlier, leaning out a window a story above me, smoking a filtered cigarette, like an actor on a break, and he peered, with his nonmilky eye, the one that never seemed to focus, directly at me. He followed me with that eye for a while and then flicked his cigarette butt onto the street between us, and we both watched it spiral down, until it hit, sending off a little flurry of sparks. Then, giving me one last piercing gaze, right in my eyes, he pulled his head back inside.

As in all tourist-drenched cities, it is impossible to walk around Kathmandu without young men offering to guide you, and as in the other places, the guide has arrangements around town to bring in business. Sometimes I try to short-circuit this loose cabal and say, "Look, I'll tip you 100 percent if you don't take me to your uncle's shop." But one young man in Morocco said, "I understand, but in this case it really is my uncle, and he will know I have not brought you, and if you could just do me this one favor, I would really appreciate it, you don't have to buy anything." Of course, I went. In Kathmandu, I was approached by an art student who offered to show me the town, and he was an energetic kid with a friendly smile and a convincing demeanor. He was good at doing basic information about the Hindu gods and incarnations of Buddha and identifying in which centuries—I mean, I assume he was right—the different kinds of woodwork that adorned the buildings originated. His art, he said, was painting, mandalas, and his master was a very great master. The kid seemed sincere. His only tell was that he backed out of any picture I tried to include him in. We eventually ended up at his art teacher's studio. There I was shown—not by my guide, but by a salesman, with my guide kibitzing—all the different thangkas and mandalas and given elaborate explanations full of scripture and story, the salesman producing a disarming and endless patter, low key but unwavering in intent.

I did like one of the mandalas quite a bit. It was, as the salesman showed me, signed, and signed by one of the few female masters, he said. She sold her mandalas exclusively through this school because she was so grateful for learning her art there. It cost, he said when I asked, four hundred dollars. I said whoo-wee, no, can't do that, which started us on a half-hour negotiation, and we landed at $120. I promised I would come back to buy it with the necessary cash.

"We can take Mastercard or Visa, no problem," he said.

"I'm sorry, I came out without my wallet," I said. "It is in the safe in my hotel room."

He looked concerned. "I cannot guarantee that the painting will be here without a deposit," he said.

I felt like saying I was willing to risk it, there were no other customers, but I just left ten dollars behind. On the way back to my hotel, I stopped in a few tourist shops and saw nearly identical pieces priced at forty dollars, meaning they would sell for twenty, and some were done with even more skill. What a thing, human psychology. When I thought I was getting it for almost 75 percent off the asking price, how could I not say yes? I let the man keep the ten dollars as a tribute to his performance and never went back.

Nepal, bordered by India and Tibet, with Bangladesh just below, is the perfect geographical spot for syncretism, and all through the city I saw Hindus worshipping at Buddhist altars, Buddhists putting garlands on statues of Ganesh, even Muslims at the shrines of the other religions. Saturday was a festival day at the big Buddhist temple downtown, and everyone was there. Thousands of people stood on the walkway at the base of the big white dome a couple stories above ground level, and thousands more walked around the temple below. People sold flowers, bracelets, statues, bells, bowls, necklaces, prayer wheels, prayer flags, incense, and burners, laid out on small stands or blankets on the ground. Teachers and healers were set up along the sidewalks and in the square too, on blankets, surrounded by petitioners. Food and drink sellers set up shop or walked through the crowd. And thousands and thousands of pilgrims circled the stupa on the several levels of walkway. The oversized dome on the top of the stupa, with its large painted eyes, made it seem as if the temple was watching all us puny humans milling about.

Only four or five percent of Nepalis are Buddhist, but on this day it felt like every one of them was happily circling the temple. As in most festival crowds milling in a space not quite big enough to accommodate them, a happy hysteria reigned, and people were in a celebratory mood. Monks and nuns were particularly exalted, feeling the respect of the multitude. The children seemed to appreciate that the adults, for whatever reason, were managing to be appropriately excited by daily life, making for a potent mixture of play and reverence. And with the various peddlers offering snacks and T-shirts and paraphernalia, it had the modest frenzy of a county fair, with a similar sense of communal enjoyment. Religious feeling turned some somber, but made most lighthearted and bighearted. People smiled generously at each other and at me.

"It is an amazing stupa," I said to a man standing next to me at one point, looking up at the hundreds of pilgrims circling it at the base of the dome.

He turned and looked kindly at me, then back to the temple.

"It amazing stupa!" he said.

Thousands of people continued to pour in and out of the square, bottlenecked at each entrance, smiling.

The woman at the front desk was happy that I was in love with Everest Momo—I'd already eaten there a few times—and suggested another place a few blocks past it, off the main drag, that served other local foods. She drew a map to show me where it was. I went up and down the street a half dozen times and asked some people on the street for help, but none of us could find it. As it got dark, I could see a room, mostly below street level, like a basement apartment, that had steam coming out and turned out to be a tiny place with a minimal kitchen—a one-burner stove, a single sink, a couple square feet of counter space, a shelf of bowls and Tupperware containers full of ingredients—and two tables, each a well-worn, stained, twelve-inch board about three feet long with a bench on either side that could seat two or squeeze three. Three diners were there, and a man took orders while his wife cooked. I sat down with two working men—I found out later that one was an electrician, one a painter—and nodded hello. Nobody spoke more than two words of English.

When the co-owner came and said something, I pointed to what the painter was eating, and he nodded and then pointed to the row of bowls, suggesting that one snack wouldn't be enough. I looked at them more closely, and one was a roil of raw chicken, one a mess of what might have been highly spiced raw beef, one of innards, a few less identifiable, all at room temp and some bubbly—oh well, fermentation is older than cooking, right? I gestured to my two new friends suggesting I needed their help, and they got it, and each pointed to a different bowl. I looked at the co-owner and pointed to those two and shrugged—he pointed to one of the unidentifiable glops, and I nodded. It turned out—I took a picture of it and sent it to my friend the food critic—that it was sheep's lung, which came fried and was a local specialty. The painter had been eating liver. Offal, the poor man's meat. It was delicious, all of it, with a Nepalese beer, although with the fried lung I had those momentary waves of revulsion we can get when we wonder what in the world we might be eating.

The painter was the communicator of my two table-mates, and we managed to establish what the three of us did for a living, how many kids we each had and how old, our opinion of this particular restaurant (all in favor), where we were all from originally (Kathmandu, the western hinterlands of Nepal, New Jersey), our assessment of Nepal at the current moment (mild displeasure, strong displeasure, abstention), our assessment of the US (pretty good, pretty good, not so good). It was one of those funny three-way conversations where two of us conversed, using nothing but our own languages and some gestures, understanding each other, while the third waited to have what I had "said" translated to him, at which he nodded or shook his head or laughed.

The cook could reach the refrigerator, her cutting board, her ingredients, her stove, and her implements without moving her feet, and her husband could hand off whatever she made to any place on either table with at most a step or two, unless he needed to get a drink from the refrigerator, which required him to squeeze behind his wife. Their deal was that she would not hand him drinks. As we all finished our food, the painter and electrician insisted I have a real drink, a rakshi, which is what they had been drinking. They poured me a shot, and I bought them one, too, I think, although who knows. I paid precious little for all of it. We raised our glasses and drank. It was clear like vodka, but a little sour, far from smooth, and high octane. They smiled as I winced a little and cheered me on to down the rest of it.

I asked the painter whether life was hard—I know, without any language in common, but as I said, we understood each other—and he looked me in the eye and admitted yes, yes. It was manageable, but yes, it was hard. We clinked glasses once more, somber as we sipped, although they laughed when I again shuddered as it went down.

ETHIOPIA

"I used to go running, in Djibouti, with the Somalis," the sixtyish man said. "They are very competitive, very fast."

He had already told me that he was Kenyan, so I said, "Kenyans don't do so bad either."

He laughed and said, "I don't run like that anymore. I don't even walk like a Kenyan!"

He was seated at the breakfast table next to mine in my hotel in Addis Ababa, a more upscale place than I was used to. He was an erect man with a military posture—he was, in fact, a career US military officer, retired, and had risen to the rank of colonel. And he considered himself an expert in the ethnic tensions and rivalries of Ethiopia. Several times, he would stop a server or guest and tell them which ethnic group he thought they were from: Oromo, Amhara, Tigray, Somali. He was usually right, and when he was, he would say, "I thought so!" As I looked at him, I thought I would never have guessed Kenya; I would have guessed he was African American, which I suppose by now he rightly was, although he'd spent little time in the states. In any case, the culture of the US military was stronger than the culture of Kenya in his bearing.

To understand Ethiopia, he told me, I had to understand the long suffering of the Oromo people. They were the most numerous in the country but had never been in power and had always been oppressed by the Tigray and Amhara, one or the other of whom had run the country, forever.

"And the Somalis?" I asked. This was how his running with Somalis in Djibouti had come up.

"Ethiopian Somalis," he said. "are a special case. They are Muslim, hard-headed, shrewd. They have an egalitarian, warlike culture."

He made these proclamations without the least shred of misgiving, with martial concision.

"They are different from Somali Somalis?"

"Somali Ethiopia is curiously undercounted," he said, ignoring me. "This too is an effect of the concentration of power in Tigray and Amhara hands. Not that the Somalis are blameless. For years the lunatic leader of the province, Abdi Illey—he has now been arrested—ran the place as an absolute madman, a thief, an I-don't-know-what, and the government in Addis Ababa let him. Abdi arrested people, then made them fight wild animals for his entertainment—yes, Roman Colosseum! Astounding!"

He sipped his coffee. He was built like an oversized duffle bag—thick and cylindrical, with a very large neck blending into a very large head, all at attention, nothing out of place, and he kept his breakfast at attention as well, moving plates and silverware as necessary into rigid alignment. He wiped his mouth, put his napkin down squarely, and continued. He had spent twenty-some years in the US military, and his accent was American, but you could still hear some of the lilt and articulation of his Kenyan upbringing—whether that was Kikuyu or the British influence on Kenyan English or a combination, I didn't have enough experience to tell. He was better spoken than your average military man, and he wasn't your average military man—he had been, in his last posting, reporting directly to the then commander of AFRICOM, the storied general William E. "Kip" Ward. Ward, one of the few African American four-star generals, was the man who had invented AFRICOM and was its first head.

"Yes, well, that's another story. The young Somali warriors," he said, "they brought the changes to Ethiopia. They are a marvelous people. Look at the Somalis in America: that Somali US congresswoman, for instance, a woman, and they are the heads of school boards, they are everywhere in state and city governments. They're not like African Americans—they are very active—they want to take over!"

He was buttering a piece of toast, put it down neatly facing its other half, and picked that one up to butter.

"But for Ethiopia," he went on—I had learned I didn't need to prompt him to keep going, he was content to hold the floor, and he spoke slowly and deliberately, like he was giving a seminar—"Jawar Mohammed is the person to watch. He is an Oromo nationalist, Islamic, an ethnic cleanser, wants an independent state of Oromia purged of all people from other ethnic groups. He is a graduate of Stanford and Columbia universities but pretends he was raised in a madrasa. 'The victory of Islam is the victory of Oromos; the defeat of Islam is the defeat of Oromos,' he says. He is very dangerous. He has been broadcasting from America, where he has been in exile—*he* says exile, although I think he just overstayed his student visa—and his broadcasts and podcasts are listened to everywhere in Ethiopia and the whole diaspora. He is coming this week, part of Abiy Ahmed's perhaps unwise embrace of all his political enemies—you know he has invited everyone home for the New Year, right?" I nodded. "The Ethiopian New Year is celebrated September 11, and," he paused and looked at me again, "yes, of course there were conspiracy theories implicating Ethiopians. But at any rate he is either coming or is already here, and I fear the worst."

The dining room was small, with six or eight tables, and one couple had come and gone, as had a group of three businessmen. So we had the place to ourselves, both facing the same way, turning to each other to talk, although most of the time, he talked straight ahead and I watched his silhouette. I wondered what our waiter, who the colonel had correctly identified as Oromo, thought of his pronouncements.

"And of course," he went on, "this ethnic business was loved by the Tigray government! The Tigray are a tiny minority, despite their clout, and they were very happy to let Oromo and Amhara and Somali attack each other and vilify each other while they got rich! We, the US, did the same thing in Iraq. The Sunni and Shia antagonism? That is our creation—in Iraq there were no ethnic or religious conflicts: it was a socialist, antireligious country under Saddam Hussein. We introduced these ideas. We encouraged them. Divide and conquer."

"Well that didn't work out very well," I got in edgewise.

"Genie out of the bottle!" He smiled. "And they are reaping that whirlwind here now too. The yoke of suppression has been broken, and we don't know what will happen next. Oromo separatists, Somali separatists, Tigray revolutionaries: maybe Ethiopia splits in four? Maybe there is a war to keep it together? Everyone is excited about Abiy Ahmed, but what can he do? He makes beautiful speeches, but a year from now, at most two, when nothing has changed? Then the people will hate him and turn on him, and there will be blood in the streets."

On the way into Gondar, I asked the cab driver what he thought of all this.

"It is good thing new prime minister stops the Chinese," he said.

"The Chinese?"

"Yes, they have too much business here, they own too much business, and it is good he stopped them."

That was what concerned him, not building an independent Oromia.

Gondar is a small city, justly famous for its medieval castles, which bring tourist trade, and therefore a large crop of hotels has sprouted. I heard music coming from upstairs in mine, which I assumed meant there was a bar or restaurant on the roof, so I walked up a few flights of stairs to check it out.

A wedding reception was in progress, and the music was from a quartet of musicians on traditional instruments. The bride and groom were tightly encircled by the fifty or so guests, the whole group hopping up and down in joyous communion. The musicians, like wedding musicians everywhere, were both in the mood and not—they had a professional distance from the revelry, but they also were experienced enough musicians to know that if you didn't feel the room, the room wouldn't feel you—and so they stayed in it enough to energize the people.

I was welcomed in, took a lot of pictures, and spent some time with a group of young men who spoke English and told me about their lives. But they would only talk until the musicians started in, when they would jump up, singing the song and dancing—again pogoing with their arms wrapped around each other. They were extremely happy, but they were not drunk, which, once I noticed it, made me realize that nobody was drinking at all.

At one point between songs, I was saying to one of the young men that is was a great feeling in the room, which I too was feeling. This was true, but of course weddings tend to be happy occasions, so it didn't mean much to say it, it was just small talk. Just then a new song started, and he started singing along happily with his friends, and just as he was starting, he said to me with a huge smile: "It's a beautiful culture!"

As I left the wedding room, I was met by a shortish man in a light gray suit, maybe in his late twenties, very taken with the professional profile he assumed he was projecting. He told me he was the events manager of the hotel, and he wanted to know what I thought of the hotel and its facilities.

"People seemed happy at the wedding," I said. It was evasive, yes, but really, what could I say: everything about the hotel, except perhaps this guy's suit, was bare-bones, economy-style, minimal, adequate, Motel 6.

"We have two kinds of weddings in Ethiopia," he said, "and this is not the best. There are Muslim weddings like this, and there are Christian weddings. At Christian weddings, everyone drinks. They are wild! They are very good!"

"That sounds great," I said. "Do you have one tomorrow?"

He looked confused.

"Tomorrow is Monday," he said.

We were standing on the open roof terrace, and the bride and groom had just headed out. There was noise and commotion on the street, too much, it started to sound, to be just the wedding party leaving.

We looked over the half wall to the street. People were lined up on the sidewalk as if they were waiting for a parade, waving flags and cheering.

"Is the prime minister in town?" I asked.

"No," he said. "It is a journalist—a very important journalist. Everyone loves him. He is from Gondar and is back for the first time in many years."

A journalist? I thought. A parade for a journalist? I thanked the events manager and congratulated him on the event and the splendid hotel and headed down and out to the sidewalk to join the throng.

Young men were running down the street with large and small flags, and behind them came a convoy of vans and pickups and a couple of larger trucks. On the largest truck a stadium-sized rock-band set of PA speakers had been lashed and was pumping loud reggae music—too loud, past the system's limits, all a bit distorted—occasionally overlaid with a speaker gleefully haranguing the crowd, which responded now and then with a cheer. The vans and cars were chock-full of people waving flags out the windows, and the PA truck, a dump truck, had twenty young men in the back, maybe more, also waving flags and dancing to the music. Young men from the sidewalk joined the others running alongside the convoy so that the parade got larger by the minute. Many of those who stayed on the sidewalk jumped and clapped and cried out.

A van passed with a picture of Jawar Mohammed, the Oromo broadcast star and separatist. The journalist! I asked people standing next to me if he was in the van, and they said no, but he will be here sometime soon, maybe tomorrow. Someone else thought maybe he was there yesterday. Hundreds of people were running in support, thousands lining the street. It was a parade for Jawar Mohammed, not with Jawar Mohammed.

The next morning, the cook at my hotel said, yes, he supports Jawar Mohammed. I said I would love to know what Jawar was saying, but when I went to YouTube, I couldn't find anything in English.

"Yes," he said, "Jawar speaks the language of the Oromo. Oromo is the third largest language in Africa."

"Is it really?" I asked.

"Yes, after Swahili and Arabic."

"But everyone in Ethiopia speaks Amharic, I thought."

"Yes, this is colonialism, we are forced to speak Amharic."

"So you want Oromo to be the official language of Ethiopia?"

"Yes!" he said, with glee. "This year! We will do it!"

The next day, the colonel told me the story about General Kip Ward, head of AFRICOM, and was truly surprised that I had not heard about him—he was at the center of the biggest scandal in the army in our lifetimes, he said.

"Everyone knew that Ward was partying hard, and you can't blame soldiers for needing to let off some steam, can you." It wasn't a question. "He'd come into town and take over a hotel, fly in women, bring in local women, his staff, contractors, who knows who, and blow through piles of cocaine and cases of whiskey. This was well known." He waved his hand in the air as if he would wish it all away—it wasn't important.

I couldn't always follow the story because there was a lot of shorthand, a lot of inside baseball, and he referred to American bases by their nicknames or acronyms, so I didn't know whether he was talking about Uganda, Somalia, Libya, or somewhere else—but the gist of it was that a crisis broke out, American troops were involved, it was all questionable—some of the troops were where they were not supposed to be officially, and so there could be PR and diplomatic blowback, and as a result people's careers and, more important, people's lives were on the line. He attempted to contact his commanding officer, Ward, because hard decisions needed to be made and made fast, but Ward had given strict orders at his five-star hotel not to be disturbed, and the colonel couldn't get through. He ran out, got in a jeep, made his way over the next couple hours from the base to the hotel in full uniform, crashed through security and slammed his fist against Ward's suite door until someone answered, and then went from room of debauchery to room of debauchery until he found the general, made him focus, got a direct order, and left.

"When the smoke cleared, Americans under my command were dead, and there was an investigation. I decided I needed to tell my story or I would be court-martialed myself. It wasn't a decision to be made lightly, but men I was commanding died while I was trying to pull my commanding officer from a five-star frat party, and I was pissed. I told the honest-to-god truth. The whole drug-and-sex truth. Well, maybe not the whole truth, but enough of it. The result was that even though they later buried all the actual facts, Ward got demoted to a two-star general and was pushed into retiring. My career was effectively over too—I'd broken the unwritten rule that you always lie to protect your commander. They reassigned me to a desk job at a base in Oklahoma and I retired."

"And so, now?" I asked.

"Oh, you know, revolving door? I'm a consultant. That's why I'm here—I obviously can't tell you exactly why."

We agreed to meet up for a drink in the bar that evening. We had several. We had too many, in fact. We indulged, you might even say, in some minor debauchery, as if in homage to General Ward. But there were no lives on the line.

Winding up the hill in a tuk-tuk, north of Lalibela, we had to get out and push it through the mud. The rains had made the road impassable for anything but 4×4s. Most of the people walked, anyway, in the mountains, and some rode horses, so these perennial mud events were just a minor nuisance. The big four-wheel-drive vehicles can whirl through—it's just the tuk-tuks that are disabled. I should have been in a 4×4, being a tourist, but I liked my driver, Moses. He worked at my hotel and drove people as a sideline. He was perhaps a con artist, definitely a hustler, but that is one of the only ways for ambition to manifest in this small town in the Ethiopian mountains, and he was ambitious.

Other ambitious young people on the Lalibela streets work a few standard cons on the tourists. They know we are suckers for education, and so they ask if we might help them buy the textbook they need for their class. The first time I was asked, I said sure, I would buy the textbook for the young man, maybe fourteen, and that he should take me to the bookstore so I could. I thought if this was a con, he'd come up with a story—like the bookstore wasn't open—but instead he and his friend, a taller version of himself, the same age, agreed merrily and walked me into town.

The store was not a bookstore—small surprise, since even with the flood of tourists coming to see the megalith stone churches, the astounding full-sized churches carved out of the living rock in the Middle Ages, the town is not very big; it would be a tiny mountain farming community except for the tourist trade. The combination souvenir, bodega, and stationery store had a small stand of books, including a fat dictionary that came with a CD ROM advertised on the cover. It was marked with a price of what came to a walloping sixty dollars in US funds. And it was dog-eared, with some dark smudges from dirty hands and fingers—a bit worse for wear. I looked over at the woman at the counter, who clearly knew, who was part of the scam, who would buy the book back from the kid for a dollar or two as soon as I was gone, and she wouldn't meet my eye.

"Expensive," I said.

"Yes," she said, with a straight face.

"Do you have a computer for the CD ROM?" I asked the boy. He either knew or intuited that the right answer was yes.

The market in Lalibela is a hundred or so vendors strewn across a hillside with their produce on tarps and blankets, a few vendors of clothes and junk and incongruous spare parts, and livestock at the bottom of the hill. The day before, a bright kid of around sixteen attached himself to me and offered to show me around the old city. A series of tiny neighborhoods ringed the edges of the market as if standing guard, only accessible by foot or motorcycle, and they were the entirety of Lalibela until a few decades ago. Inside the old city, people lived in small, two-story structures cobbled together with the techniques and materials of centuries past. *This is a house*, my new guide said to me many times, as if even he had a hard time believing it. He had, though, he said, grown up in the old city himself.

We talked about what everyone in Ethiopia was talking about then, the new prime minister, Abiy Ahmed. He had come in like Obama, as a hope and change candidate, and as one who would heal the wounds of a society riven by ethnic conflict and the long domination by that small ethnic group, the Tigray. Like Obama, he was the product of a mixed marriage, his mother and father from each of the two largest ethnic groups, the Oromo and the Amhara. Ahmed, with his half-and-half heritage, represents in his person, like Obama, a bridge across the divide. It was a thrilling time to be there, and everyone, from the monks in the hills to the children in the street to the academics and taxi drivers, felt the momentousness of the change.

One of Ahmed's first acts was to unilaterally end the twenty-five-year war with Eritrea by granting it a hundred percent of the land that had been in dispute and over which the countries had ostensibly been fighting for decades. On New Year's Day, I met my friend Elias Wondimu, who had gone into exile some twenty years earlier. He had been a journalist at a time when journalists were being systematically jailed and even murdered by the regime; he went to a conference in the US and decided, at the last minute, that it was unsafe to return. While in the US, Elias had started Tsehai Press, publishing books for and about Ethiopia and the Ethiopian diaspora, was a professor at Loyola Marymount University, and had become an important figure for the global Ethiopian community. When the new president visited the US soon after he was inaugurated, one of the people he sought out was Elias. As part of Ahmed's campaign of reconciliation, he had invited the entire diaspora home for the holiday; Elias of course came. It was his first time home in more than two decades.

We met and went to his cousin's house on the edge of the city and had the first of too many, too abundant, and superb meals we would have that day. We watched on TV, with his cousin and his family, as Ahmed met the dictator of Eritrea on the Eritrean border. They hugged each other. Hundreds of soldiers from the two armies that had been fighting each other for twenty-plus years laid down their weapons and hugged each other; and then citizens from both countries ran into the former battlefield and embraced. My friends were in tears— "We never, never thought we would see this day," Elias's cousin said to me.

The kid in the market, though, as he took me around Old Lalibela, was blasé about it all.

"This PM," he said. "Yes, he believes in love and peaceing. Maybe that will work."

"You don't sound very confident," I said.

"I'm not. It is Ethiopia today, it will be Ethiopia tomorrow. They will find a way around him."

"Who is they?"

"The army, the ministers, the rich. And he doesn't put his enemies in jail. Big mistake."

The old city—maybe "city" is grandiose, since it stretched just a few blocks in any direction—had a bar stashed every couple hundred feet, all of them identified by a stick stuck in the ground with an upside-down can capping it. It was daytime, so the men lounging in these makeshift places were by definition day drinkers. Many of them, sitting on logs and stones and the occasional chair, half inside and half out, looked to be in bad shape, with glazed red eyes, ragged clothes, and patchy skin. They did not look happy to see me walking by either, and I noticed my guide moved faster as we passed. Some of the women cooking and cleaning were not that happy either, and I moved us back into the market.

"You see," the young man said. "Our problems are not just Oromo–Amhara or Ethiopia–Eritrea or Tigray–Somali. People are poor. What can we do here? Just be farmers and monks and drink all day, or be modern people, join the world? I don't think the PM can help us with this."

We had run into the mud as Moses was taking me to see one of the most important monasteries in the country, at the top of the mountain just north of Lalibela. Every once in a while, I got out and walked as he slid the tuk-tuk through the mud, alternately got it stuck and unstuck, stomped the mud off his feet, and picked me up. As we started back up the hill, I told him what the kid in the market had said, and he said, no, that was all wrong.

"We need to do business, not politics, and anyone can do business," he said. "We don't need the PM, we only need God's guidance and blessings. I have my job at the hotel, but I also drive, I own this tuk-tuk, and when I buy a van, I will drive more people, and then I will start my own hotel and have guides for the people, and a restaurant. I can do a big business, with God's help."

He had what struck me as a very nineteenth-century combination of beliefs: a trust in both self-reliance and a

Calvinist divine plan. He spoke of the monks with great respect, and he said a few things that suggested he was impressed by their learning, even though it was not for him, being a businessman. We got to the end of the road, thousands of feet above Lalibela, and walked up to the Asheton Maryam Monastery. He bowed deeply to the monk and reminded me that I needed to tip him because he was the head monk, the most important scholar.

The night before, Moses had convinced me I needed to go to the best restaurant, the most interesting place, best view in Lalibela, he said. I should let him drive me, and I would not regret it. The restaurant was owned by a Scottish woman who had come once just to visit and decided to move to Lalibela and start a business. She was a model for him, although much older, and a mentor, and I would be impressed, he told me, as, "with God's help, she has made a very good establishment."

I went that night—in Moses's tuk-tuk, even though his per-mile fee kept inching up—and the restaurant was a crazy collage of spaces, with oddly shaped platforms at many different heights, up and down the hillside, and metal stairways, many of them curved, going from one to the other. It was anything but slick, built by people who of course had never done anything like it before, and looked like a rough sketch of what it was supposed to be. All metal and concrete, none of it made much sense or had any flow. Each platform had one or two tables, and to get from one to the next required going up and down and around—madness as architecture, madness as restaurant design.

I sat and ordered a meal and some wine. And there was another tourist perched across from me, too far to chat, and two Ethiopian women a few platforms away, although whether they were local or tourists, who could say. The man got up and left, and I started to notice that every time I glanced in the women's direction, they were looking at me, and each time they smiled, I smiled back, but I didn't want it to seem like I was looking for a date or assignation, so I immediately went back to my book and meal.

After ten minutes or so, one of them came over and demurely asked where I was from. I said the US, and she said they were students in the university in Addis but were home visiting their families.

"I don't want to bother you," she said, despite the fact that she did want to bother me. "But are you here on business?"

"No, I am a professor," I said, "at a university in California," hoping to suggest a professional distance. "What are you studying?"

"I am studying biotech and my friend is studying mechanical engineering." The friend, I had noticed, was still sitting a few pods away and smiled when I looked over.

"Would you and your friend like to join me for a few minutes?" I said. "I'm just going to finish this glass of wine and go home, but there is some more in the bottle I'd be happy to share."

She waved her friend over and motioned her to bring their glasses.

"What can you do with biotech in Ethiopia?" I asked when we all were seated, because engineering, well everyone needs engineering. The restaurant we were in could use some engineering.

"The agriculture ministry would be the only place.

There is nothing here for me really. How long are you staying in Lalibela?" she asked.

"I'm leaving right away in the morning," I said. "I'm flying to Djibouti."

"Why do you go to Djibouti?" the friend asked, truly curious.

"I just thought it would be interesting," I said. "Do you know anything about it?"

"Is there something in Djibouti?" the biotech woman asked, and then answered her own question. "There is nothing in Djibouti."

Her friend agreed.

"Yes, there is nothing in Djibouti," she said.

I wrote down my name so they could friend me on Facebook, and I wished them goodnight.

As I went downstairs, the Scottish woman was there, and I chatted with her briefly about her life and the development work she was doing in town, most involving girls' and women's education, as it turned out. While we were speaking, Moses came in to find me.

"Ah," I said to the Scottish woman. "You know Moses, I think!"

She looked up at him with a slight frown. "Yes," she said. "I know Moses." With that and a curt goodbye, she walked back into her office.

Wow. It was pretty deep shade, from a woman he had cited as a mentor of his, but my polite questions to him about it in the tuk-tuk on the way home didn't get me anywhere.

The head monk, at the top of the mountain, was grateful for my contribution, and he offered to take me to see the monastery and church, with Moses as interpreter. A Chinese computer systems engineer, around twenty-eight or so, joined in with us as we went. He was working on a project in Addis for his Chinese company and would be living in Ethiopia for three years, which was fine he thought; he got significant hardship pay for it. It became clear in talking to him that he was a Sino-supremacist, and although I wasn't Chinese, he assumed that, as a white person and therefore from a relatively "advanced" race, I would agree with his assessment of the myriad deficiencies shown by the rest of the races of the earth. He took no hints and didn't seem to hear the retorts I made. I shrugged when I realized it, and he didn't notice that either.

The monk was a sweet guy with a quiet demeanor and deep, expressive dark eyes. He grew up on the mountain and from a young age was attracted to the monastic life. On the way up the muddy road, as I hopped in and out of the tuk-tuk, I had met a number of the children who lived up there—they were interesting, these few who met my gaze, with a self-containment and curiosity perhaps both bred from the same isolated existence. The monk had turned all that curiosity toward the realms of spirit and history. It was hard to tell at first what his discourse was like since it was filtered through Moses and so sounded much like Moses, who also added his own commentary.

"He says this is a chalice from the twelfth century, and you see it is gold. I can't imagine—can you?—what such a thing is worth in today's money."

But the monk had a soft voice and communicated a deep love for the place and the artifacts under his care. He showed us a number of chalices and staffs from the twelfth and thirteenth centuries, and I could see he was just as enamored with their patina and significance as he had been thirty-five years earlier as a novice. The Chinese engineer grabbed at the relics and turned them over in his hands, which I could see worried the monk, but he waited and when the engineer was done, gently put them away in their cases and holders. The monk and I had a fine conversation, through Moses, while this was all happening, and atheistic though I am, I fell in love with his love of his life on the mountaintop, surrounded by these endowed tokens of divinity and history.

The pièce de résistance was a twelfth-century vellum New Testament, which he gingerly brought out of its box. Moses was very impressed.

"He doesn't usually show people," he said. "Just the box." And it was true, I felt we had made a bond, the monk and I, looking at each other as Moses intervened.

He opened the volume to a couple of the pages, some illuminated, lettered with a fine Amharic script, and the engineer reached out and grabbed at a page, pushing forward, trying to flip ahead—the monk was going too slow for him—and I said, "Please, don't touch it!"

"It's okay," he said, "I'm careful"—he wasn't—and pointing at the monk, he added: "He goes too slow." I felt helpless. "Please," I said. I couldn't tackle the Chinese man—that too would be disrespectful in the stone sanctuary—but I couldn't manage to shame him, and the monk, pained, seemed to have no experience with a tourist this sacrilegious. His eyes expressed more sadness than concern as he put the book away, and he didn't bring out any more manuscripts.

That night, I went to hear some traditional music at a small bar, and Moses, again my driver and translator, explained to me what I was seeing and hearing. The place was dark, and so unless the musicians were right in front of you, it was hard to see them. Two different couples, looking like they were on dates, sat across the room, and one table of loud people was drinking a lot. They, along with the two of us, made up the whole audience. Moses explained that I must tip the musicians, and when I did, they came over and sang a very long song, ten minutes or more, composed on the spot, about what a good tipper and generous person I was.

Back in the hotel I heard some chanting as I was falling asleep, coming from the street, but I faded out. I woke up at 3 a.m. to hear the chant still continuing, sounding much louder in the quiet of that hour. It would get closer and then farther away, then faint, before getting closer again. I could hear one woman most clearly, although other voices joined in. She sounded desperate, angry. I went to the window and looked out, couldn't see anything, but could now hear that it was one woman wailing and the other women crying. I went downstairs. The desk clerk was sleeping on a couch in the lobby. He woke as I walked by, and I said I was worried because someone was in distress outside. He said yes, it is a woman in the neighborhood whose husband had died, there is nothing to do, they are mourning with the family, they are honoring the dead.

I woke again at 6 a.m. and realized I had been hearing it on and off in my sleep all night. I went back to the window as the sound grew closer again and could see that six pallbearers were carrying a coffin as a group of mourners walked in front and behind the casket, wailing in grief, yelling incantations, in extremis. This chorus of lamentation had been circling the block all night, carrying the dead husband on their shoulders, their anguish undiminished.

Moses drove me to the airport later in the morning. I told him that I wished him the best of luck in building his business.

"With the help of God and his angels, yes, I will succeed," he said.

"You have a lot to live up to with your name," I said. "You need to deliver your people from their current woe."

"My name?" he said. "Yes, it is from the Bible."

I hear from Moses occasionally, now that I'm back home. He gets in touch on Facebook and by email. He has a very florid writing style:

> Dearest my blessed Tom, I am here saying many thanks for your last familiar email. Of course, there is nothing as pleasure than assuring the wellness of friends and family. So, I am so happy to receive news and to assure your wellness. In fact, you are such a humble flesh that lives in the will of God and can imagine as you will always be in the guidance and protection of the lord.

We exchange some notes on our respective families, and I try to get some information about the politics of the moment, but he is not a political person—he wasn't interested in politics when I was there, and either isn't paying attention, even as things deteriorate now, or not interested in writing about it.

I did however talk with an Eritrean cab driver in San Francisco some months after I returned, and he was worried. The Oromo nationalists had been having violent demonstrations at the urging of Jawar Mohammed and others. More than a hundred people had died in demonstrations in recent months. He was very knowledgeable about Ethiopian society and politics, and I wondered how he knew so much. Could he watch Ethiopian television when he was young?

"No," he said, "no, no, no. We had no telephone, no contact, no crossing, no nothing. It was war, always."

"How do you know so much, then?" I asked.

"You know, I am here now, World Wide Web," he said.

I talked about being there for New Year's, and the Ethiopians crying when they saw, on television, the reunification of families on the border of his country. He said, "Yes, we thought it was forever war."

He had been in California for ten years, had been back just a couple times—he came legally, so if he has the money, it is easy to visit. He wasn't sure which place felt more like home anymore. Maybe California. We talked a while about Djibouti, agreed it was a terrible place, and he said I would love Eritrea, especially the capital Asmara. I asked if the same ethnic divisions made for tension, and he said no.

"You have Oromo and Tigray and Amhara and . . ."

"No," he said, "no ethnic differences."

"Everyone is . . .?"

"Just Eritrean."

"Huh," I said.

"Well, yes, some small tribes of different people in the mountains here and there, true."

It isn't true. Around thirty percent of Eritreans are Tigray, who are the same group, and speak the same language as the Tigray of Ethiopia, and there is a related group almost as large, and seven or eight others. But, as my colonel had said, without someone to rile up the groups against each other, they did not—at least many did not—experience those differences as fundamental or fraught.

I said that one thing I noticed in Ethiopia was that the Somalis don't seem to get involved in these ethnic political battles, and he explained that Somalis—in the Somali part of Ethiopia, 95 percent of the people are Somali—are just waiting to rejoin Somaliland. This is the desire, the wish, the goal. They don't care about Ethiopian politics because they see themselves as leaving.

"Wow," I said. "That seems strange to me—Somalia? Who would want to be part of Somalia right now? A broken state, unbelievably poor, why want to be part of that?"

A big smile broke across his face. "Yes," he said, in prideful chagrin, "Africans are crazy."

"And your dictator in Eritrea, how old is he?" Isaias Afwerki has ruled since the war of independence in 1993.

"In his seventies."

"If he's like Mugabe, he could have twenty more years!"

"Yes, we hope not. He is not as strong as he was. People want him gone. We will see."

Moses, in his last email, finally responded to my questions about the political situation.

> The actual situation is not good currently, there are organized groups in some part of the country and some of them are using different propaganda and creating division in every ethnic groups. There has been female students kidnapped in the oromia region. They were kidnapped due to their heredity and this has brought serious conflict. God has solution for everything and let us pray to have such a peaceful world.

The worst thing that could happen for the region, my cabbie in San Francisco thought, was for Abiy's coalition to fall apart, for Jawar Mohammed to win the election and split Ethiopia up. Then war, he thought, would start again because it would be good for both governments.

"Terrible for the people," he said, "but good for the governments. They make people afraid." Our eyes met in his review mirror. He smiled. "But maybe not. Maybe Abiy wins, we get rid of Afwerki in Eritrea, and brotherhood!"

Now, as this book goes to press, war has broken out between the Tigray People's Liberation Front and Abiy Ahmed's government, causing some twenty-five thousand refugees to flee across the border to Sudan. Some foreign policy experts suggest that, as in the case of Yugoslavia, without a repressive strongman regime, the ethnic federalism that has been the hallmark of Africa's second most populous country is doomed. Between the violence and the pandemic, tourism has all but ceased, and the people I met have needed help to get by. Ahmed has gone from winning the Nobel Peace Prize to using his air force to bomb targets within his own borders. A small ethnic group in the far south has also declared independence. It remains to be seen whether Ethiopia as it has existed for the last century will endure.

MARSHALL ISLANDS

y first stop in the Marshall Islands was Kwajalein Atoll. My plane touched down to let off and take on passengers, but only US military personnel and military contractors were allowed to deplane. As we landed, I could see people playing golf at a course that bordered the landing strip. Gray military buildings and radar antennae and the golf course took up much of the island. Fighter jets and transport and observation planes were parked everywhere. I watched the life of the base—the workaday jeeps and the golfing—go on for half an hour and then we started taxiing off again, and Kwajalein, or Kwaj, as it is called, receded, the oddest island in the South Pacific, all paved, institutional, industrial-complex gray blandness except the palm-lined fairways and greens.

Even the poorest Micronesians have enough food—coconuts, taro, bananas, and other fruits grow everywhere—but not the Marshallese. They don't have enough land to be able to feed themselves. Kwaj is the largest island in the group, and it grows nothing but the few coconuts that fall from the golf course trees. Nothing that grows on Bikini Atoll, one of the outlying islands, obliterated by twenty-three nuclear bomb tests in the 1940s and 1950s, is edible because of radiation—

the largest above-ground blast the US ever caused was on the island. The rest of the Marshalls' thousand-plus islands are spread across 750,000 square miles of ocean, which makes it larger than any country in Europe. But it is comprised of only seventy square miles of land, seven square miles of it paved over on Kwaj, and a fair amount of the rest sand and volcanic rock, with only forty-some square miles available for agriculture. Five percent of that arable land is on Majuro, where some twenty-seven thousand people—half the population of the atoll—live. If every square inch of all the islands were cultivated, including the airport, roadways, and beaches, it could feed at most a fifth of its residents.

Seen from the air, Majuro looks like what it is, the thin remnants of the rim of a huge volcano. In most places the island is a city block across, in some just the width of the road or wholly submerged, in other places as much as five or six blocks. It is a tiny place, even if the road is some twenty miles long, all told. Shortly after my touch-down on Kwaj, I landed at the single-runway airport on Majuro, which had perhaps fit comfortably on the island during World War II but had required some filling in of the lagoon to make it wide enough for today's aircraft. The runway sits two feet above sea level and crumbles on the edges into breakwater rocks. The ocean, calmed by a reef a half mile off, licks at the shore. It's hard not to find that ocean, however calm at the moment, slightly threatening, especially under cloud cover when the sky turns gray and the water turns dark.

My cab driver from the airport told me that his village, on a nearby island (nearby, that is, using South Pacific standards—it was four hundred miles away), had a population of five hundred; only twenty, he said, had paid employment, all at either the municipal offices or the schools.

"But we have taro, coconut, banana, and fish," he said. "Also some of us work here and can buy things people need. We are okay."

On Majuro, the island, home of Majuro, the nation's capital, where he worked, many people were visibly not okay. There is an alcohol problem. Unemployment is chronic. People are not happy.

I asked the driver whether he had noticed the water rising at all because of climate change. Yes, he said, definitely, the water was higher. He wasn't sure that it was time to panic, but it was noticeable.

There are not many restaurants on Majuro. At one of the largest ones I met two young American women. They asked me what I was doing there, and I asked them the same. I said I was on this United Airlines flight 155 trip, stopping in a half dozen islands across the Pacific.

"Well, you've hit the most exciting one of all now," one of them said. "No, just kidding."

"But are you kidding?" I asked. "Is there anything to do?" I wasn't looking for tourist activities, I was just wondering what it was like for two young women, fresh immigrants to this very quiet, depressed place.

"No, there is nothing to do," she said. "Nothing." She was not complaining, just giving the neutral fact. I had assumed they were military or government, but they were both teachers. One was on a year-long contract and had two months left; the other, a two-year contract with a year and change left. They both were somewhat stunned. They had each flown off the island only once since they arrived—one to Pohnpei and one to Kosrae, other islands in this multination chain across the Pacific.

"Sometimes it's fun to watch people play basketball or volleyball," the other said. "It comes to that."

"Is there a restaurant that serves Marshallese food?" I asked. They look at each other.

"No," the one said.

"No," the other said.

"Why did you decide to do this?" I asked. "Why come here to teach?"

"I really don't know," the one said. "Seemed like a good idea at the time."

"And you?" I asked the other.

"No idea. I had just gotten my master's. They needed teachers."

"People are nice," the first one said. "They will get up and do things to help you unexpectedly—shoo a menacing dog away in the alley, see that you are lost and give you directions. But they aren't entirely, I don't know, not entirely chatty."

I had noticed that too.

"In Micronesia," I said, "it's hard to walk down a road and not end up in a conversation, but not here, it seems—but I've only been here half a day."

"Early in the morning, people are chattier," the other said. "Before it gets hot."

The infrastructure is better than on Chuuk. I said that to a man working at a restaurant, and he nodded. He was from one of the nearby islands, but I couldn't tell whether it was the same as my cab driver's.

I asked him how things had changed in the four decades since he was young. When he was a boy, he told me, there was no electricity on his island, only kerosene lamps.

"Have things changed here, on Majuro, too?" I asked.

"Yes, now everybody has cell phones."

"Some of it looks much better than Chuuk," I said. I told him about the road in Chuuk, that it was terrible, and that the main section had been under construction for years.

"Yes, that road, it was being built by a company from here," he said. "They didn't get paid, so they quit and left. Never got paid."

"Someone else is doing it now—I think Chinese," I said, and he shrugged, as if wishing them better luck.

"But here it seems like people are doing well. I've only been from the airport to here, but the road, the houses, they seem in good shape."

"Yes. Good people. Good times. Look," he said, pointing to one group on the side of the road, "Sitting talking to friends!" and then, pointing to a woman with a young girl in her lap on a front porch across the road, "Or telling stories!" He said this last with an appreciative laugh.

"Yes, nice," I said.

"When I first came, thirty years ago," he said, "very few cars. Now everyone has a car, builds house. Yes, it is good."

"Is the water level different?" I asked. "You, know, from global warming, climate change?"

He looked confused.

"The water at the airport, especially," I said. "It looked like it was about to flood the airfield."

"No," he said, "no different. The water has always been right there. We are an island. We are right in the water, always that way."

I grabbed a couple bananas at a mini-mart. Pointing to the cover of a magazine showing the disastrous aftermath of a typhoon, I asked the woman behind the counter when it had happened. The woman glanced at the magazine, shrugged, and waved my question away. "There is one all the time," she said.

It was impossible not to feel the fragility of the islands and the fragility of lives—to feel the deadly weather and the sense of subjugation. Spain had claimed the islands at the end of the sixteenth century, sold some of them to the Germans in the nineteenth century, all of them were granted to Japan after the First World War, and the Americans took them after the second. Although the Marshalls were granted independence in 1979, the US retained the entirety of Kwajalein, which the Marshallese are forbidden to visit; not even the people who were displaced from there, their land appropriated by the US military, are allowed on the island unless they have jobs on the base, and almost all of them must live on a neighboring island and take a ferry to work. And the Bikini Town Hall is a daily reminder of superpower abuse—it sits in downtown Majuro because it cannot be on permanently irradiated Bikini Atoll. Have these villainies made the Marshallese hard? Or is it the seemingly perpetual dependency on the US? The islands use the US dollar (although perhaps about to be replaced by a cryptocurrency), the US Postal Service, the FCC, and defense forces, and rely on US aid for a full third of their GDP. Or is it the impossibility of a decent life for half its citizens, given persistent, astronomical levels of unemployment? Or, related, is it the skewed income distribution? For people like my cab driver, things are good and getting better. For a lot of the young people, not so much.

"Half the adult population is unemployed," one of the teachers said. "That's why it feels so desperate. And with poverty, of course, everything that comes with it."

"There's a new female president, though," the other said. "Initiatives on domestic violence and things like that."

"There's just not enough local food," the first said, "and the imported is incredibly expensive."

"The young unemployed men," the other said. "They are a problem, like everywhere that is poor."

And I would see that over the next days. Many of the young men—twenty to thirty-five—looked a bit surly and dissipated, with chips on their shoulders, like lost Rust Belt kids, riding around in beat-up cars getting high, pissed off, with no options anywhere. They didn't want to talk, and some had all the signs of alcohol damage.

"Church is good," the other teacher had said, returning to our earlier conversation, "as a thing to do." So on Sunday morning I spent several hours in a church. On all the islands, music is important, and there is at least one ukulele in any group of five or more people, any day of the week. People spontaneously harmonize, and everyone knows the traditional songs. Just walking along, you hear the sound of a few people singing together, the sweet sound coming out a window in perfect harmony, or at a restaurant, a large table of friends or family will start singing, and knowing it will happen, someone will have brought a uke.

At the church there may or may not have been a separate choir, or maybe the people who stayed the longest all just sat near each other, and everyone sang. Each person picked their own part and went with it, building complex, ethereal harmonies on the fly. The service itself was improvised, and the congregants came and went as they pleased. I asked a man there my climate change question.

"Oh yes, definitely," he said. "The water is lower. Not like when I was a kid. Now, very low, lots of times."

Walking through a small neighborhood after church, I heard music coming, weirdly, from a large shrub. I ducked my head in and a group of seven or eight boys were hanging in its branches, one playing a ukulele, all singing, except one eleven-year-old doing a beat box accompaniment. They sounded like angels, doing five or six different harmony parts, just hanging out of the heat, full of boyish joy at their own sound. I stayed for a few songs, taking pictures—they were happy to have the audience—until a man came out of a nearby garage and yelled at them in pissy Marshallese, and they all scattered. I don't know whether the man yelled because he knew I was there or not. The boys, when he started yelling, seemed like they had expected it and were quick to bolt.

The next day, I caught Flight 55 again, headed for my next island.

"We will be beginning our descent to Pohnpei shortly," the pilot said two hours later. "We've been notified that there is no water at the airport currently, so you may want to use the restrooms on board before deplaning."

So much water everywhere, and such minimal plumbing. So much paradise, and so much trouble getting by. The disagreement about whether the sea level has been going up, down, or neither is so human—how do we gauge things? How do we know what we know? How far does our belief determine what our eyes see? Does what we expect make our future what it is? Do I find kindness because I expect to?

Well, yes, and of course not: climate change is real, the hydrogen bombing of Bikini Atoll was real, the continued occupation of Kwaj is real. People can be right or wrong about these things without changing them. But kindness—how do we gauge that? What is paradise? Here we have only the eye of the beholder, the heart of the beholden, the act of receiving, the act of believing, an expression of kindness, an expression of gratitude— and although these are all just as real, we have no Geiger counter, no yardstick to measure them. Only, as I say, the eye, the heart, the act, the expression.

BANGLADESH

On the flight into Dhaka, the woman sitting next to me was from New Zealand. She was in Bangladesh, she said, to help the Rohingya refugees, working for the UN.

Her job, which seemed arduous to me, was to help coordinate the 150 different NGOs on the ground in the refugee camps south of Chittagong, and to help get funding from governments around the world.

"The difficulty isn't the job," she said. "It is really just the misery." Sometimes, when it gets to be too much, she escapes home to New Zealand.

"Or sometimes," she said, "to anywhere that isn't here."

She had worked in a number of places doing the same thing, most recently in Iraq.

I asked her if she had any say in where the UN sent her.

"Oh, I don't actually work for the UN—I'm a contract worker. I applied for this post, just as I had applied for the ones before. So when this contract is over, I'm back looking for work again."

She had dirty blonde hair and the tan and lined face of a surfer, and that vibe too, a tough, tomboyish, unconventional person of thirty-five or so, who looked able to throw a punch or lead an army, and more likely to be found just about anywhere than in a traditional office job.

"And how will you find the next contract?"

"Same way," she said. "They post the positions they need filled, the UN, on their website, and you just put in for them."

There were a lot of people like her, she told me, because most of the work that the UN does like this is staffed by stringers, and many of them get to know each other and bump into each other in new hot spots.

"So you've run into some people from Iraq here?"

"Iraq? Maybe . . . But you do see the same people—a woman is moving into my building now that I knew in South Sudan nine years ago. And I have a South Sudan dog with me that she helped me neuter back then!"

"So you do wars too, not just refugee situations."

"Well, they're the same thing, just a matter of how close to the fighting you are. But I stay back a little anymore," she said. "I'm done with being in the middle of war zones—I saw enough of that in Sudan and Nigeria."

"Will you burn out on this work too? Do most people just do it while they're young?"

"Well, I guess you'd say I'm in my third wave—war work, then emergency work, now admin. I don't do hands-on work with people anymore, and I suppose that's the burnout factor, the people. Now I'm just talking to the people doing the hands-on work."

"But as you said, it's hard to face the misery—do you think you'll have to move on from this too?"

"No," she said, quietly. "I guess I'm an emergency junky. We're all a bunch of emergency junkies in this line of work. We're misfits, really."

She looked sad as she said this, pained. I got a sense of the wound below the extreme competence.

"And I'm not sure, frankly," she said, "what else I could ever do."

Lalbagh Fort is a tourist attraction, and as at most of such sites I visited in the Bangladesh, the vast majority of tourists were from somewhere else in Bangladesh. I saw two people of European descent the entire time I was in the country, besides the woman on the plane, and neither of them were tourists—both were working in Dhaka, both seemed to be long-time residents, and both looked like they were on their way to a meeting. The tourists at Lalbagh were ninety percent Bangladeshi, and ten percent Chinese. This was good for me because, being an outlier—being one of a kind—I was of interest, and it was easy to meet people and talk.

Lalbagh is a seventeenth-century Mughal walled complex, with a beguiling pink central tomb (of Pari Bibi, a Mughal princess) with a reflecting pool leading to the front and round turrets in each corner. The tomb, the two-story governor's mansion, and an orange stone mosque are set in roomy, flat imperial grounds. At the fort I became a popular prop for family and school group photos, and for the first time in my travels, more people asked if they could take my picture than the other way around—this was a change that had been in the works over the last decade with the growing ubiquity of smart phones. I got in a conversation with a group of college students about American politics and was surprised when one kid said he loved Trump. It was so unlikely, so unexpected, that I waited for an opportunity to talk to him one on one.

"I was surprised when you said you liked Trump," I said.

"Everyone hates Trump," he said. "I just say maybe he isn't so bad."

"He hates Muslims, though," I said. "He hates brown people . . ."

"Yeah, I know, I just don't like the bandwagon, when everyone already agrees with something. It makes me uncomfortable. Group think, right?"

"Yeah, but in this case . . ."

He laughed and said, "Yes, I know. I'm just that guy. I can't go along with the crowd."

"What did you think of Obama?" I asked.

Without hesitation, he said: "*Obama was a god!*"

On the street, young men sell books. They walk between lanes of traffic, a three-foot stack of trade paperbacks in their arms, and sell to drivers and passengers through the windows for cash. These are pirated books for the most part, and one boy, seeing that I looked American, pulled out Michael Wolff's *Fire and Fury*, which had only been out for a month in the US. He also had Obama's *Audacity of Hope*, Karen Armstrong's *History of God*, Dan Brown's *Inferno*, Walter Isaacson's *Steve Jobs*, an Orwell, an Ishiguro, a Hosseini, Kahneman's *Thinking Fast and Slow*—I was impressed by the reading tastes of the driving public.

The traffic is so jammed up that drivers have time to scan the stack and do a transaction before they move again. They may even have time to read some of it later during the drive, when traffic stops dead yet again.

I had seen the Bangladeshi Parliament building in a documentary about its architect, Louis Kahn, and it was my one specific goal in Bangladesh, the one place I was dying to see. Getting around Dhaka is tough because it is a maze of streets, lots one-way, nothing parallel for long, and it is enormous, the metro area twice the size of Los Angeles and its city density off the charts, almost twice that of Hong Kong or Mumbai. It's a density you feel every minute on some streets—especially in Old Dhaka, where the combination of pedestrians, bicycle rickshaws, horse-drawn wagons, cars, trucks, and tuk-tuks keeps every available spot on every available street at capacity all day. Other parts of the city are less congested, but the traffic is incessant everywhere. I took tuk-tuks rather than taxis because they could slide around some traffic jams, which meant sucking a lot of exhaust and compressing my spine bump by bump, but less time in the snarl.

On Monday morning, I set out to see the famous building. The Parliament is in Sher-e-Bangla Nagar, a neighborhood just northwest of Farmgate, but I had a difficult time getting my driver to understand where I was going. We drove around for an hour or more and didn't ever seem to get there. I didn't know the Bengali word for "parliament," and that didn't help; my phone's map had transliterated street names so that didn't help. There is a Sher-e-Bangla cricket stadium about two miles north of the building and a Sher-e-Bangla mosque a mile or so south of the building, and as usual, the traffic was so knotted it took half an hour to travel to each of those spots. I got out at the mosque and tried a new tuk-tuk.

After a couple of false starts, he dropped me at the entrance to the parliament grounds, the building still a ways off, and I took the long walk to get to the gate in the 90-degree sun. Halfway there, guards stopped me from going further and sent me to a kiosk, which was empty. They signed that the man would return after lunch. An hour later, he came and I got in line behind a half dozen others. When it was my turn, he told me he was sorry, but Parliament was closed. I said I just wanted to walk around the grounds, but he said it was impossible. I should come back tomorrow, he said.

The next day, it only took an hour to get to the entrance, and I stood in line for half an hour as a number of other people got their passes. When it was my turn, a new man asked for my papers, and I gave him my passport. He looked at it, handed it back, and shook his head no. I asked why, and it seemed that nobody in the kiosk that day spoke English. I started asking the people coming and going if someone could translate for me and found a man who could. As we walked back to the kiosk, I told him what I wanted to do, and without even talking to the kiosk he said, oh, no, Parliament is always closed on Tuesdays.

"But I was here yesterday, and the man said to come back today!"

"I'm sorry," he said. "Perhaps you misheard."

"No."

"Perhaps he misspoke."

"I guess so."

"Tomorrow?"

He said something to the man in the kiosk, who answered.

"Yes," he said. "Tomorrow."

On Wednesday, the man in the kiosk, with the help of a translator I flagged down, let me know that Parliament was in recess. He didn't know when they would resume, maybe tomorrow.

The building has a number of Khan's signature shapes, many large circles, many circles in squares, but most striking, a kind of moat that makes the entire building look like it's floating, the signature achievement of a singular artist. I could see the building, about a quarter mile away through the grounds, but I couldn't make out any features, couldn't see the water. It looked great, but it looked better in the film. Of course, the camera was able to get much closer than I managed to do.

On the banks of the Buriganga River, large ships were docked, ocean-sized ships, ready to ferry people across or take them upriver. Small wooden skiffs plied the waters, full of passengers and goods. A tiny motorboat with an improbably large stack of boxes pulled up to one of the big ferry boats and unloaded its cargo—whether it was for onboard use or further transport, there was no way of knowing; a crewman kept one foot on the ferry, one foot on the skiff as the boxes were handed off, and then the skiff headed back across the river.

A young man who spoke English came over to ask where I was from. He asked if I'd like to come on a boat, and I said sure. He talked to someone at the top of a ramp and then motioned me to follow him. We hopped onto the ferry and walked around. Some families had set up camp on the football-sized lower deck, some on the upper, a hundred feet long, forty feet wide, blankets on the ground, luggage around them, sharing a picnic, and two young men had a hundred ducks under a big net in the back, with a tarp strung over them. I pointed to the sun and to the ducks and shrugged, to ask whether it was to keep them from getting too much sun, and they nodded yes. They talked to the English speaker, who told me, yes, they have trouble keeping cool, the ducks, unless they are in the water. I asked where they were taking the ducks. Upriver, they told him, where they lived.

I told him about the trouble I had getting to see the Parliament building.

"The problem is that you do not know anybody. In Bangladesh, you have to know someone to do anything."

"Can you help me get in?"

"No, I don't know anyone either. Here at the docks I know people; that's why we could come on the boat without a ticket. But"—and he smiled at the idea he might—"I don't know anyone in Parliament!"

As I walked down the street at about 10:00 p.m., a number of men in bicycle rickshaws offered, as usual, to drive me wherever I wanted to go. As I told one persistent guy that I was just out walking for my health and did not and would not want a ride, I noticed a bespectacled man in his late forties clock us and stop fifty yards ahead of me. He was carrying some plastic bags of groceries and a briefcase, but he put them down on either side of his feet. He looked like an accountant, nerdy, domestic.

As I walked toward him, I said hello, and he said hello back.

"You need to be careful," he said.

"Oh?"

"Yes, some of these rickshaw men, especially with tourists, especially at night, are up to no good, no good at all."

"Well it is very nice of you to look out for me."

"I am very happy to, sir. We are a very good city of very good citizens, but there are always a few bad apples. Is that not always the case? We would not like you to have a bad impression of us."

"I don't have a bad impression, I have a very good impression," I said. "People have been wonderful." His hair was slicked down with a part on the side—part of what gave him that pocket-protector, accountancy-office look.

"That is splendid! Do you mind me asking where you are visiting from, sir?"

"From Los Angeles." As we talked, he sometimes gestured out toward the city, as if directing attention away from himself, and kept his gaze around thirty degrees to the left of me, steadily enough that I once turned to look over my shoulder to see if some ne'er-do-well rickshaw driver had caught his eye.

"A superlative city! I would very much like to visit someday."

"I do hope you will, sir, and that people will be equally kind." I said. I had found myself picking up his formal diction, some Pavlovian imitative gesture.

"My house is just a few blocks from here," he said. "My wife would be very pleased to offer you a cup of tea."

"That is very kind of you, but it is quite late already, is it not? I would hate to impose on you or your wife."

"Perhaps then tomorrow?" he said. "And it would be no imposition, but a great honor for us. Allow me to give you my card. If you are at a hotel nearby, perhaps it wouldn't be too much trouble?"

"You're very thoughtful, sir," I said, "thank you." I wondered for a second—is there a chance he knows someone at the parliament building—but decided it was too long a shot, and too odd a question. We said our good nights. It took around three hyperpolite exchanges to get it done. But he was very kind.

DJIBOUTI

The flight from Addis Ababa to Djibouti touches down in Dire Dawa in the middle of the desert, many miles of brown away from lush Addis. Pure aridity stretches from there to the coast and the port city of Djibouti. A near-solid regime of tan.

Port cities often have an air of desperation, as if Sidney Greenstreet and Humphrey Bogart might be holed up sweating somewhere, one or both of them drugged or shot. Djibouti is the ur-port city, a place that has no reason for being except that it is a port. Everyone is coming or going, and only a few solid citizens and the desperate who can't leave don't.

Djibouti calls itself the "Dubai of the Red Sea," suggesting a booming city, growing in stature and importance. It is true that it is the most important city on that stretch of coast, but that isn't saying much. The only city of any size between Djibouti and the Horn of Africa is Bosaso, a fifth its size, and in the other direction there's only Port Sudan, half its size, until, a thousand miles north, you hit Suez. The economy is fueled in part, as it has always been, by shipping and smuggling but also by its strategic position and the resulting major international military presence. Both France and the US have enormous bases here, but they are self-contained, with their own shopping and services and supplies, and in the city you see few Western military personnel. The airport looks more like a midwestern airport in the 1960s than anything in the Emirates, and much of the city is still a run-down version of itself, tarnished and dilapidated, its glory days behind it. It is many, many hundreds of sparkling high-rises short of being the next Dubai. It doesn't have even one.

The airport is a scene of chaos, with a lot of yelling, many taxi drivers and customers upset about something. I was rattled by the level of vehemence and asked my driver whether this was on the meter—he had a meter on the dash—and he said yes. I didn't notice until we were halfway to the hotel that the meter wasn't on, and when we got there, we had a heated conversation in French about how much he wanted to gouge me. I ended up paying him what he demanded but not without calling him a *lardon* and also not without thinking that, okay, I see why everyone is yelling at each other. It turns out that *lardon* means brat; I was remembering *larron*, which means robber; I'd meant to call him a *voleur*—a thief, a gonif.

The country is the size of New Jersey, with less than a tenth of the population, and it is desert, with nobody and nothing past the city limits except a few goatherds and some scattered villages. And the city itself has no sights, no attractions, and yet sky-high hotel prices— keyed to arms dealers, military contractors, and Pentagon visitors, ludicrously high for this part of the world. I settled on a motel that was $170, even though it was a mile and a half from the city center, because it was less than half the price of the others. It was in a bit of a wasteland—no lights, and the sun had set an hour and a half earlier—with low-level industrial and storage buildings, more tin than concrete, for a half mile in any direction. Even the motel was scarcely lit and looked like a warehouse.

I checked in with a charming, tall man with graying hair and an Omar Sharif moustache, who wished me a pleasant stay. At 8:00 p.m. it was 95° F (35° C), and I was sweating from the heat and my angry argument with the cabbie. The office was open to the outside, and the people there didn't seem bothered by the temperature; I was looking forward to my air-conditioned bed.

A young guy grabbed my backpack and took me to a room. It was small, it was dingy, it had a single bed in it that had an almost nonexistent mattress and a minipillow, but I thought, whatever, I've slept in worse. I turned on the air-conditioning unit on the wall and looked for Wi-Fi. No signal. The A/C unit didn't seem to be working, but I figured I'd give it a chance and went out to where I thought the restaurant was. There were just a couple of guys drinking tea. Omar Sharif was gone. The boy behind the counter didn't speak English, and he either didn't speak French or couldn't understand my terrible accent. At any rate, the restaurant was closed, the nearest one was in the city center (which was communicated by pointing), and there was no traffic on the road, much less a cab. Oh well, I thought, I can stand to lose a pound or two.

Back in the room, the air conditioner was making noise and moving a tiny bit of air but was not cooling it at all. I sat and sweat while I wrote up some notes from the day, slapped at some mosquitos, and thought, okay, enough, and took my pack back to the front desk and asked for a taxi. The taxis are called taxis, of course, and have TAXI written all over them, and so there was no mistaking the request, but the boy looked a little panicked and just said no.

"No taxi?" I said.

"No taxi," the kid said, without affect.

I pointed to the phone. "*Appel le manager*," I said, and he hesitated. "*S'il vous plaît, monsieur,*" I said, "*appel le manager.*" He got nervous. "*Maintenant,*" I said, stabbing at the phone, "*S'il vous plaît.*" He broke down and called.

Omar was gracious and charming and said he would have someone in to fix the air conditioner tomorrow or the next day and that he was sorry the restaurant was closed and the Wi-Fi not working, they were making some upgrades, he was sorry for any inconvenience. I asked him to call a cab and suggested that given that nothing the Expedia description said about the place, down to the picture, was at all accurate, he might want to refund my money.

"That is impossible," he said.

I said, "Okay, just a cab, then."

"I am very sorry, sir," he said, "but taxis will not come out here in the middle of the night."

"It is 8:30," I said.

"Yes, it is impossible."

"And the restaurant is closed."

"Yes, for renovations, it will be open next month."

"When did it close?"

"In the past," he said. He had sensed I was making a case and so was getting a bit cagy.

"Well, I think you should refund me, but either way I'm going to the Ambassador Hotel."

"Yes, this is impossible. I am so sorry our renovations have inconvenienced you."

"You seem like a pleasant man, but I have to say I think you're wrong. Expedia, who I paid, said the hotel had a restaurant, A/C, and Wi-Fi, and it has none of those things. Plus the room is filthy and the bathroom rusty."

"I am terribly sorry, sir. There is a no refund policy."

"Is it your hotel?"

"Yes, sir."

"So you write the policy."

"Yes, sir, and I'm afraid that is the policy. How would we stay in business if everyone who asked, we gave back their money?"

The phone was making my ear sweat even more, and a drop fell from my nose.

"I think you should make an exception," I said. "*Bonne nuit.*"

I shouldered my pack and went out to the street. It was dark for as far as I could see in both directions. I started walking toward the city. Once in a while a motorbike went by in the other direction, the driver staring at me, and once a man, sitting on the sidewalk, leaning against a building, appeared out of the gloom. He took no notice of me, which made me think he was drunk or high or waiting for me to have my back to him. I glanced over my shoulder for a couple blocks, which didn't help in the darkness; he was lost in the shadows. The heat hadn't let up at all and I was soaked—the pack was heavy, and I found myself hoping I was going in the right direction, since I didn't seem to be approaching any city, still no glow to be seen. I was jumpy, on the lookout for desperados, sweating, my clothes soaked, my crotch chafed, not quite in a panic but close.

This, I thought to myself, *this is why people think you're crazy, this is why they don't know whether to laugh or shake their heads when you tell them stories about your travel. Why would anyone put themselves in this position? Why would anyone want to be here, now, walking for miles in the steaming black night, surrounded by poverty and desolation? What is the point of all this?*

A half hour later a few lights showed the beginnings of a neighborhood. Five or six more blocks in, a street had some life on it. And there, parked on the side of the road like an oasis, was a taxi. I walked up to it and a middle-aged man in the passenger seat waved me off. I walked around to the driver's side, and a very young cabbie looked up at me without rolling down his window, with a look of fear in his eyes. I wondered for a minute whether the passenger had him hostage, but I was too hot and beat to worry, and made the international sign for *roll down your window.* He did. I said, "*Où est l'Hôtel Ambassade?*" and the man in the passenger seat leaned over and tried to give me directions. I tried repeating them to him but kept getting it wrong, and then, exasperated, he motioned for me to get in.

He told the cabbie in French to take me to the hotel, and the young man started the engine and began to inch out of the parking spot only to pop the clutch and stall the engine. Then I saw why the kid was panicked. It was his father in the seat next to him. He was getting a driving lesson. The first one, judging from how inexperienced he was with a clutch. A few stalls later we were underway, and with some lurches and some yanking on the steering wheel and yelling by the father, we arrived at my hotel. He waved off the cash I offered once but took it on the second proffer.

I paid my $350 for a dingy old room at the Ambassador and turned the A/C on, started to fill a rusty bath—the place was almost a dive, but the A/C had dropped the temperature down ten degrees, and it was so many grades above Omar Sharif's motel that I was thrilled. Out the window, I saw three or four people tucking in for the night on the sidewalk under a shop awning, their cardboard beds still there from the night before. I thought about finding something to eat and turned off the bath. There was no hot water, but that was okay. I took a grateful cold shower, laid on the bed, and slept the sleep of the dead.

The next day, I walked around the city, which is divided into a "European quarter" and an "African quarter." It did occur to me that this only makes half a city, but it is probably just a bad translation from the colonial French *quartier*, or district. The European quarter had a few remnants of a better past—a few signs on the sides of buildings that would have been glamorous when they were applied in the 1960s but were now missing enough letters that it was impossible to figure out what they used to say; one was $R - - - - R I - R A - - S - L$. The colonial architecture was crumbling into chalk, jumbles of wire hung from poles, the streets were so potholed they were reverting to gravel, and although there were dozens of men sitting in the couple of cafés in the center, there otherwise wasn't much of the business action you would expect in a capital city—Djibouti is a country, Djibouti is its capital. Okay, I thought, then the African quarter must be where the shops and office buildings are.

But no, the African quarter was cordoned off by an extended souk, full of merchant tables and stands, a little medina, and it was hard to figure out how to get to the other side—I eventually slipped through a curtain and walked in. The severely rutted dirt roads were smaller, the women were all in chadors or niqabs, the buildings were single story and run-down, and there was even less business than in the "European" part of town.

I found a fish restaurant, though, and went in. It was tiny, with a few chipped Formica tables and a refrigerated chest against one wall, the owner a winning man who looked Somali and looked happy to see me. I pointed to another diner's fish—a small whole fish—and the owner opened the refrigerated chest and mimed that I should pick one. I pointed, somewhat at random, and sat. A soccer game was on a small-tube TV mounted on the front wall. A violent argument broke out between the customer with the whole fish and the proprietor, apparently about what he was being charged. The shouting went on for quite a while and continued to accelerate, enough that I thought actual violence might ensue. It made me wonder whether, as a normal way of doing business, I should have been yelling at Omar Sharif the night before. Clearly yes.

Whatever transpired between the two of them, it wasn't enough in the customer's estimation. He left fuming, yelling, and throwing his arms in the air.

My fish came, a whole fish butterflied and slathered in a hot spice mix—pepper, cumin, cardamom, sumac, maybe something else—cooked in a very hot oven, so the skin on the bottom was burnt, the top browned, a tandoori-like effect. It was served with a banana-based mash that was an unappetizing gray but delicious, with enough honey that it countered the almost overly spiced fish perfectly. It was the best meal I'd had in weeks, in this unlikely shack. Another diner got in a verbal fight with the owner, but I thought, no big deal, just the way it goes down here, and who cares when the food is this good. The flies buzzed around, but not too aggressively, and I left nothing behind but the clean fish bones and fins.

I got up and thanked the owner and was surprised when he asked me, in English, how I liked the Yemeni food. I said I didn't realize it was Yemeni and praised it to the skies. I asked him what I owed him, he told me, and I did the math. $60. I was expecting, based on every-thing I'd eaten in the last month, for it to be $6. I laughed and said you can't be serious. Oh, yes, he said, you picked a very expensive fish. I said, come on, really. He smiled pleasantly. I told him it was bad for business, that word would get around, and he would get no more business. I wasn't yelling, like the last customers he gouged, I was just saying.

"No, no sir, it is okay, it is $60."

"But think—I will tell my friends to never come here. You could become a must-go-to restaurant for tourists, but not if you take advantage of people like this."

"It's okay," he said. "I am already must-go-to. I am in *Lonely Planet*. $60."

He smiled. He was unperturbed, unperturbable.

I walked back to my hotel, happy to get out of the heat and dust and decay.

PERU

What to make of the walls of Cuzco? Are they unthinkable, or is it just difficult to think there, since so little oxygen gets to the brain?

The air was so thin that we were zombied out, which we knew would happen, and we were doing everything we were supposed to do to counteract it. We came up slowly on the train rather than flying in—supposedly, this helps one acclimatize because the train is slow, climbing and switching back a dozen times to scale the mountain, the sea-level city below shrinking with each leg. We drank as much coca tea as we could because that was supposed to help and because we thought maybe, if we drank enough, we'd get a little buzz. But sitting in an outdoor café in Cuzco having yet another cup, I noticed L——'s eyes start to dim and flutter, and I was afraid she'd pass out. I started to get up but was too slow. The waiter, who had seen a lot of this in his time, was way ahead of me, and he caught her before she took a header from her chair.

We had checked into our hotel—something L—— had chosen, a bit chichi for my taste. One of several hotels there that are built into the mountain, its rooms were almost like caves, one or two of the walls, sometimes even part of the ceiling just the living rock, and we went back with the idea of sleeping it all off, hoping to wake up acclimated. But in the middle of the night we woke up sick unto death, throwing up, diarrhea, and not just the regular *tourista*, but colonoscopy prep-level, fire-hose weirdness. Equitably sharing the bathroom was a charged matter. We didn't know if it was altitude sickness or food poisoning or something else, but we were in agony, moaning, and carping like little babies, *oh, oh, god, I can't stand it, let me die, wah, wah, wah*—giving each other permission to act like dyspeptic toddlers—just pitiful really, no filter, no shame, just a festival of horrid bodily noise and effluence punctuated by vocal self-pity that went on for hours and hours. We finally fell asleep at 4:00 or 5:00.

At 8:00 the sun was streaming in and we woke, trying to remember where we were, and we heard a slight swishing sound. And then a small cough.

We looked at each other. The walls that weren't rock were so thin we could hear the people next door turning over in bed. And we realized at the same time that we had forced them to listen to us cussing and whining and erupting, heard us heaping imprecations on god's head, heard our every whine and bodily function for three-quarters of the night. Each horrendous moment of the last eight hours came galloping back on the steeds of shame. Did we dare go down and have breakfast? Could we stand to face the people we had tortured—and undoubtedly disgusted—all night?

The walls of Cuzco.

The stones.

They are big—so big it would take twenty men, maybe more, forty men and levers and pulleys and—what, giant screws?—to lift one. They are irregularly shaped, with multiple angles. They fit together so flawlessly you could not slip a piece of paper between them. Some of the stones weigh two hundred tons. They are a puzzle.

I've done a little stonework, a little brickwork in my time: walls, veneers, chimneys, countertops. Making pieces the right shape, even if you have the buffer of a half inch of mortar to hide the less fortuitous swipes of the chisel, is tricky. Brick is softer, at least, but hard stone, like the granite of Cuzco, is difficult to shape, difficult to chisel and not crack, difficult to cut, even with electric tools and diamond-coated blades. To stand contemplating the jigsaw walls of Cuzco, this giant's three-dimensional jigsaw puzzle, is to experience a profound disorientation, to ponder one's basic assumptions about human history and human capability. *Chariots of the Gods*–style alien intervention theories, aluminum foil hat–wearing, Area 51 conspiracy nut ideas I'd always scoffed at—their gravitational pull got stronger than I thought possible. How did the Incas do it? Some of the rocks weighed two hundred tons—four hundred thousand pounds. How did they move them? How many times did they need to lift them up to rechisel each surface so they sat flush? How on earth?

But I was still altitude sick, or maybe food sick, jet-lagged, not entirely in my right mind. Besides, I was listening to a guide talk to a group of tourists, free-loading, a tour parasite, and he was moving back and forth between a scientific, historical, materialist view of things and something much more mystical and shamanistic, channeling the Inca worldview of spirits and powers undreamt of in our philosophy. I found myself transfixed by the famous twelve-sided stone, lost in the disappearing millennia....

And then to slam back into the modern earth in Lima—
what a depressing city. It sits out on a barren plain that
slopes for miles down to the sea, like a place shunned
by nature and culture, left on its own on a desolate, gray
shore. Walking down a street in the city center, bustling with shops and sidewalk stands, I was cased by
two teenagers. They turned and pretended to look into
a shop window when I clocked them, but they were on
my trail, and they split up like wolves so one was on each
side of the street as they stalked me. It was the middle of
the day. I went into a bookstore and spent a half hour,
thinking that would shake them, but they were there,
waiting, one a block down from the bookstore, the other
across the street, pretending, the minute I emerged, to
be immersed in something—the one on my side reading
a flyer, on the other window shopping yet again.

And the entire city is paranoid. Not only are there
coils of barbed wire on every wall along the street and
pieces of broken bottles cemented into every surface
that might be climbed, even twelve stories up, balconies
were booby-trapped and iron-grated, garlanded with
razor wire. The sense of besiegement was universal.
The two kids stayed on my tail as I dodged in and out of
stores, trying to keep a few paces ahead of the thieves—
because, now an hour and numerous blocks into this cat-
and-mouse game, they could be nothing else—and they
could see that I knew what they were doing. They didn't
care. I was the lame wildebeest, separated from my herd,
and they just bided their time, waited for their moment.
They were disconcertingly sure that the moment would
come. After several more blocks, I made a mad dash to

my hotel. I told L——the story, and she asked if we could get room service for dinner.

How to think of such violence? Because nobody strings razor wire on a tenth-story balcony without a strong fear of violence, a fear that must come from experience. The Shining Path guerillas, Maoist revolutionaries, bombed and kidnapped and coursed fear through the country for years, and that must have something to do with it. The natives and the colonizers have been at war, sometimes with guns and sometimes with laws, as throughout the Americas since the fifteenth century, and racism and poverty and oppression resulted in both the Shining Path and in a plague of street crime. So, no surprise. I shouldn't have been surprised.

The next day, we got a cab at the hotel and took it to the Larco Museum, a collection of pre-Columbian art most famous for its erotic ceramic statuary, with thousands of figurines fucking and sucking or just standing with gigantic genitals, erect penises larger than the figure's torso, vaginas twice the size of the woman's head. It was more disquieting than fun: nothing about these totems suggested pleasure, and they weren't clinical. I couldn't put my finger on why, but they were disheartening, not a celebration of sexuality but more like a porn addiction, equal parts compulsion and sadness. Again, was it just my mood? Then I came across a series of glass cases full of fired clay figurines—like the others, six to twelve inches high, displaying all manner of grotesque venereal diseases, and thought, no, it's not just me, this is dark. Who makes such art? These were not medical school dummies, they were not for instruction, they were art just like the other pieces, with the same exaggerations and variety, just diseased, pustulating, blistered, tumored.

From there we went to the Museum of the Inquisition, and as at all displays about the Inquisition, one despairs at the species. You can do nothing but miserably gaze upon the human being reduced to its foulest essence.

We got a cab back to the hotel and along the way I saw a sign for a playa, a beach. I asked the cabbie if it was a nice beach, and he smiled and said yes, beautiful, and then caught himself and glanced in his rearview mirror.

"Oh! For you? No," he said in Spanish. "For me it is beautiful, but for you, no, it is too dangerous. You cannot go there, I'm sorry."

"Not even to drive by?" I asked. "Just to see?"

He shook his head. "No," he said. "It would not be prudent, no."

We went back to the hotel and ordered room service.

The guide I was eavesdropping on as he explained the stones of Cuzco asked us to think about the civilization that would build such walls. It was a civilization, he said, that was far, far advanced technologically. No culture anywhere in the world in the thirteenth century (or the fourteenth or fifteenth or sixteenth, for that matter) had the capability to construct walls with twelve-sided stones so massive and do it so impeccably that, as the rampaging conquistador Francisco Pizarro's brother said, you cannot slide a pin between them. The Incas had perfected not just this but the most sophisticated accounting systems the world had yet known, and they made metallurgical and other advances. They represent one of the great flowerings of human endeavor. But think, he said at one point, about how violent their neighbors must have been for them to feel the need to build such massive defenses, and to do it all so far up in the mountains, as if making a last stand against hordes of enemies. And this was well before they had any idea that the Spanish would one day arrive to decimate and destroy it all. And, although he didn't say this, the whole group couldn't help but ponder this juxtaposition: the height of civilization, the worst of humanity.

And from there, like every tourist in the world lucky enough to get this far, we went on to Machu Picchu, to stand in the dripping clouds and marvel anew.

What can I say about Machu Picchu? It is like walking into a calendar photo. So few places look exactly like the best pictures of them ever taken—Machu Picchu does. And it would take a heart of stone not to feel the sublime in full force there. It is sublime, it is what the idea of the sublime was developed to describe.

Beyond that it has none of what I look for in a place. There is no culture: the culture there died some eighty years after it was built in the fifteenth century, perhaps because of conquistador-transmitted smallpox. And there is nobody to talk to. Locals are there now just to service the endless parade of tourist buses that climb the switchbacks up to the site and the endless stream of hikers walking in. They had their fill of talking to tourists years ago. So it is a kind of silent retreat, a place to walk and wonder, to commune with the Incan mysteries, to be surprised, repeatedly, by vertiginous glimpses down the steepest mountains in the world, to experience a rare combination of the natural and the historical sublime. That is a lot, but that is all.

It is sublime.

NEW ZEALAND

hree young Maori, all in their twenties, stood by the front door, the woman in a feathered coat, the men shirtless, their shoulders tattooed in the traditional style, all wearing short skirts. They were on a break, smoking cigarettes, between shows at the Waitangi Treaty Grounds, a national monument a hundred miles north of Auckland. The Treaty of Waitangi is the foundational document of New Zealand as a nation, first signed in 1840 on the land where these performers stood smoking. As documents of native dispossession go, it was pretty good. The performers were part of group of twenty or so who demonstrated traditional Maori music, singing, dance, and ritual for the small crowd of tourists who file into a wooden-benched theater two or three times a day.

The performances include a lot of ritual enactment of battle, a dance in which the young warriors act as warlike as possible, wielding spears and clubs and grimacing in order, as it was explained to us tourists, to dissuade any potential enemies from picking an actual fight—it was dance as deterrence. The choreography involved a lot of foot stomping, a lot of lunging forward, menacing, angry chanting, and muscle flexing.

But offstage, the kids were anything but warlike. Three of the youngest of the troupe stood off to the side between shows, and I got a sense they thought of themselves as countercultural. They were not sullen, but they weren't animated either. More diffident than cool, maybe even depressive, sucking on their cigarettes away from the rest of the company, outcasts. Or maybe they were just young people working a demeaning job—every day they use the same stale material, brandishing their spears and baring their teeth to the oohs and aahs of one credulous, gullible audience after another—like carneys, losing respect for humanity one day at a time, praying that none of their high school classmates ever comes to the show....

Deep into the countryside, the day before, we had driven in search of a small motel we found online. We didn't have a reservation, and they weren't answering the phone. A gamble, but it sat next to a bird sanctuary we wanted to visit, and it was part of a working farm, so it didn't occur to us it wouldn't be open for business. When we arrived, the parking lot was empty, and knocking on the front door wasn't rousing anyone. It was surrounded by quiet pasture and forest, with few businesses of any kind within miles, much less other places to stay. The phone signal had petered out, and we flipped through a guidebook trying to figure out where to go next. As we did, a young woman came out a side door and explained that the couple who had been running it had retired and moved to Auckland. Their son was going to open it back up for the season—when was the season? Not then, apparently—it wasn't open now.

The young woman had an accent, and I was going to guess Italy, but in fact she was from Mexico. She was an artist, and her practice was taking old crockery—teacups and saucers, gravy boats, and salad plates—smashing them with a hammer, and then photographing the results.

"So the artwork is the photograph," I said.

"The artwork, I think, is the whole thing," she said.

She had met her boyfriend in London and came back with him when he took over the farm and inn. They had been living in New Zealand for just over a year. She called him while we were standing in the empty parking lot, and they discussed what to do with us. They decided they could put us up in one of the detached cabins—we just wouldn't have any service, they said, and no food. We'd have to fend for ourselves, but we could rent the room for the night.

We were grateful and dropped our stuff in the room. We walked the mile or so to the bird sanctuary, a four-square-mile fenced forest of awesome ferns and vine-bedecked trees. The flora were labeled, and viewing platforms climbed up the largest trees. There were conspicuously few birds. We ended up talking to a woman in her seventies who was a volunteer there, and she was surprised when I mentioned how scarce the birds were. She had seen a whitehead not long ago, and we spent some silent time scanning the trees. Nothing. Up on the viewing platforms we stood, silent in the canopy three stories off the ground. We heard a couple birds, but we didn't see any.

When we returned to the farm, we found the scion, a sweet young man, earnest and open-faced, with light blue eyes, very white skin, and unruly red-hair, and he insisted we come into the main house and have dinner with them.

"How did you find the bird sanctuary?" he asked.

"Beautiful. No birds to speak of. . . ."

"They're trying!" he said.

He was a music therapist and had just spent his day with a number of autistic kids who were his clients, and we talked for a while about his job. I have a friend in Los Angeles who does the same work, so I was happy to hear about his methods. I noticed that, just like my friend, he was a quiet, thoughtful, easy-going guy, and they both found working with the autistic kids endlessly fascinating, the human mind on an autistic tilt displaying a beautiful combination of human genius and human obduracy. We asked him about growing up here, in the middle of gorgeous nowhere. Twenty years ago, he said, there were even fewer tourists, and his parents only rented a couple rooms—like all their neighbors, their main income was from farming.

The dark-haired Mexican broken-crockery photographer-artist and the red, white, and blue Kiwi music therapist were a study in blooming youth, both alive to the world and ready for anything. They weren't married, and they weren't thinking about it; they were very comfortable with each other.

I told him about what appeared to me to be the enormous difference between Australia and New Zealand and their relation to the original inhabitants of their land. We had just come from Cairns, where the Aboriginal people we saw seemed downtrodden, some living on the street and many not much better off. One of the first times I was in the American South, in Charleston, South Carolina, years ago, I said, I saw an old African American man crossing the street downtown who barely lifted his feet when he walked—as if having absorbed the blows of so much racism, he was literally bent over and slowed down by it. The Aboriginal people in Cairns had that look too, as if their backs were warped earthward by the rain of racist contempt, their heads bowed, eyes averted. None of this, I told our red-haired host, did I see in New Zealand.

"Yes," he said, "The difference is we're all mixed here. We were never clannish, like the Aussies—the Maoris were not clannish, and the settlers were not clannish, never had that all-stick-together idea. We were mixing from the start."

"What percentage, do you think, are mixed?"

"Near about all of us," he said. "Like me. I'm Maori."

"No you're not!" I said into his light blue eyes, his wild, bright red hair, his white skin under the sparse red beard.

"Oh, yes, my mother's mother was Maori, my father's father some, and like I say, probably all of them some. We're all mixed."

"In Mexico too," his girlfriend said, "we are very mixed."

"But still, there are problems in Mexico," I said. "Prejudice against indigenous people, and against immigrants from Guatemala and El Salvador—am I right?"

"Yes, problems. But not as bad as US or Australia. And here, it is true, it is not problems. Here is much better for me than US."

At the treaty grounds, the older performers at the Maori culture show seemed considerably less conflicted than the younger. They did their job with equanimity, with the self-assurance of middle age. I talked to one woman of around forty after the show and asked her how she liked working there. Very much, she said. She was glad to be able "to pass on the history and culture of her people." It was rote, but she looked me in the eye as she said it, and I wondered whether the young performers, smoking their cigarettes across the lawn, would one day have her comfort and confidence. I had to assume they would, if they stayed, because why wouldn't they?

Sitting on the beach south of the treaty grounds, outside my cheap seaside motel, in the quiet gloaming at the end of the day, I remembered my UN emergency worker on the plane to Bangladesh, and how she would come back here, to New Zealand, when the stress and strain of her job got too heavy to carry.

"You have family," I had said, as a prompt.

"We won't talk about that."

"I get that."

She looked up at me, like perhaps I might be considered one of them, one of the people for whom home is not the goal.

"Friends, then?"

She considered this, and made a funny scrunch with her face, half frown, half smile, like the cartoons of chagrined people with a squiggle for a mouth.

"There is something about the place," she said, after a pause. "It isn't home, but it's more like it than anywhere else."

The woman who ran the motel—and I mean ran the motel, doing the check-ins, the laundry, the books, everything—had a similar attitude. She wasn't from this town where she worked, she said, but further in the countryside, and her smile made it clear she was happy to be there. The young Maori dancers too—it wasn't a great job, but it was good enough. And the volunteer at the bird sanctuary agreed there weren't many birds, but there had been a whitehead, not too long ago. It's hard to argue with a culture that finds, in what it has, enough for the requirements of the day.

BHUTAN

My guide and driver, like all the guides and drivers in Bhutan, wore traditional dress—the *gho* is a bathrobe-like, knee-length, often striped garment secured with a cloth belt, with extra-long sleeves that role up or down depending on the activity and the weather. Bhutan sells its traditions cheerfully and well. Each year, 250,000 tourists (and growing) come to the tiny kingdom of 750,000 citizens, and each year the kingdom trains a new crop of young guides and drivers, making sure they know their history and the dharma and how to fix a flat tire.

The only way to visit Bhutan is through an officially sanctioned tour company, and they manage everything from the minute of your arrival until your departure, including your visa, your hotels, and your meals—a friendlier version of the old Intourist routine in the Soviet Union, which, as in that case, helped insure that no tourists strayed from the approved path. It is anathema to my sense of travel, but there is no other option, and so I did it. And I found it oddly relaxing. I get, now, why people allow themselves to be taken on tours. I still will never do it unless under duress, but I get it.

Ugyen Wangdi, my driver, and my guide, Pema Sonam, were polar opposites. Bhutanese use two first names, most of which can be used for boys or girls, no last names, and there are only around fifty names, total, in use. They can go in either order, so there are many people named Pema Sonam, Sonam Pema, Ugyen Wangdi, Wangdi Ugyen, Pema Wangdi, Sonam Ugyen—all this is confusing for foreigners since at least two percent of the population is named the equivalent of Richard John and two percent named John Richard. They referred to each other as Mr. Pema and Mr. Ugyen, just like they called me Mr. Thomas.

Landing at Paro airport requires the plane to take a hard right turn between two mountains, thrilling from the air and even more exciting to watch from the ground, the jet narrowly clearing one mountain to lower itself into an implausibly narrow, L-shaped canyon leading to the airport's single runway. Pema and Ugyen picked me up and took me directly to a festival underway at the Dzongdrakha Temple, with an audience of a few thousand people, all locals except for me and a scattered handful of other tourists—it was low season. A troupe of fifteen or twenty dancers, many wearing two-foot-high demon masks and elaborate costumes—half Chinese opera, half Bhutanese peasant culture—all festooned by dozens of tiny painted papier mâché skulls. A second group wore simpler costumes and played drums and cymbals. It is story-dancing, a histrionic reenactment of both historical military battles and mythic battles against demons. It wasn't exciting narratively, and the choreography was ritually repetitive, but that didn't matter. This was an enormous communal picnic, people on blankets on the hillside, sitting cross-legged by the hundreds in front of the dancers, leaning against

the temple buildings—big stucco edifices in the style of
Tibet's Potala Palace, the walls tapering slightly as they
rise, halfway between an Egyptian angle and square, an
angle that I always find thrilling, I'm not sure why.

Pema was a sharp, fit young guy, maybe twenty-five,
although he already had two kids, and he was wound
pretty tight. He ate beef at every meal I paid for, could
never get enough of it, but he didn't eat as much on his
own dime, he said—it was expensive. Mr. Ugyen was
closer to forty, and he was quieter, more reflective, a
sweet guy who talked to his children every couple hours.
His wife had left—Pema told me, with Mr. Ugyen listening—he didn't know where she was, but she was gone,
so he needed to care for the children, and he wanted to
apologize for having to talk to them while he was driving, and I said, of course, no worries, please, tell him, I
said to Pema, to talk all he wants.

Pema held forth with aplomb—he had been a good
student at his guide school (we bumped into a guide
school lesson one day, as we were seeing one of the
sights, with thirty young adults learning how to describe
the place from an experienced guide, all of them going
silent and melting into the scenery when we showed
up), and I imagined Pema to be one of the guys in the
front of his student group, raising his hand. He was
unplagued by doubts either religious or existential. The
way it was was the way it was, and he saw no reason
to entertain any other version of the universe than the
one he had memorized, all two hundred Buddha stories included. He was conventionally pious, spinning
every prayer wheel he passed, and had the wary, hungry

confidence of a young man who had sometimes been called handsome by young women. His hair was either gelled or in a permanent cowlick.

I asked to eat one night in a less touristy place than those we had been visiting. Many of the restaurants serviced the tourist trade almost exclusively, although some had an upstairs-downstairs arrangement so the guides and drivers could eat more cheaply—once in a while, when Pema was eating with me upstairs, he would ask for the downstairs meal instead if it was beef and the upstairs meal was not. Mr. Ugyen consistently declined my invitation to join us, I assumed so he could spend lunch talking to his kids rather than us. They brought me to a woman's house, a humble, lived-in place, where we sat on the rug and had tea as she went about the business of getting us dinner. She had the bored and efficient ways of someone who did this for a living, and as each course and each convention was explained by Pema, I started to understand that this was one more stop on the tourist route, that the woman of the house was in the tourist business too, offering an "eat in a local home" experience. Even so, it was more relaxing and interesting than the restaurants.

"Mr. Ugyen says he would like to talk to you as well, that you don't have to talk just to me," Pema said.

"Oh! You speak English?" I asked. I had no idea—he had never made any sign, never nodded in agreement or shook his head in disagreement, nothing.

"Yes," Pema said. "He speaks English. He is just quiet."

Ugyen smiled at me.

"I didn't know!" I said, and he did the Bhutanese version of the Indian head waggle. I started asking him the questions I had asked Pema earlier—where was he born, about how he managed as a single dad.

"I am sorry," he said. "I need to call my kids all the time."

I assured him it was fine, he should never worry about it. "Is their mother involved with the children too?"

"No," he said. "I don't know where she is." She had left with another man. "He had more money," he said with a sad smile. "Maybe they are in Europe. I don't know."

"Was he European?"

"No," he said, and after a pause: "just rich."

"It must be hard for the children," I said.

He was slow to talk, not just because it was painful, but because he was innately reticent and thoughtful. "Yes. They do not understand." He shrugged, as if to say, *how could they? I don't even understand.* His reserve had turned eloquent. "But now it is two years. We are normal now." He laughed silently. "This is why I have to call them and tell them to do their homework while I am driving."

Bhutan is a monarchy and every business and every home has a picture of the king or of the king and his family or both. This home—over the most imposing piece of furniture, a large hutch—had a photo of the king, his wife, and two children, posed in front of a backdrop of autumn leaves, the kind of photo you could have had taken of your family in the 1980s, with the same garish technicolor saturation of color. And they looked like a TV family, an idealized group, like 1990s Sears catalog models: the king dully handsome, the queen unobtrusively pretty, the kids conventionally cute and unmemorable, and all of it unmistakably modern, much more Megan and Harry than Queen Elizabeth. And though they wore traditional dress in the photo, their hair, their attitude, and their pose were all very up to date, or if not exactly up to date, at least very 1990s.

In many different places around the country, I had seen pictures of the king's father and the king's grandfather, of his great-grandfather and great-great grandfather, back into the sepia, unfocused past. This king's father, Jigme Singye—the king is Jigme Khesar—had abdicated at the age of fifty-one and passed the throne to his then twenty-six-year-old son. Jigme Singye's father had died when he was only sixteen, so although he abdicated when he was still quite young, he had already been king for thirty-five years. Jigme Singye's father and grandfather had both died in their forties after reigning twenty or twenty-five years, so he had outlived and outreigned them both; his great-grandfather, the founder of the modern monarchy, had reigned for only twenty years. So he decided it was time.

Jigme Singye was a modernizer. He oversaw major improvements in education and healthcare—leading to drops in maternal and infant mortality, raising school attendance from 20 to 97 percent—and ceded much power to a democratically elected government. The son's modernizing is a continuation of his father's. The most striking difference between father and son is this presentation of the royal family as everyday people, people with a modern look and outlook, communicated through the staged informality of many of the images—images that are everywhere, on billboards along the roads, for instance, even deep in the mountains. The message is clear: tradition is important, but we are modern people.

How did they feel about living in a monarchy? I asked. As always, Pema answered while Ugyen thought.

"The king is a great king, as was his father. His father invented Gross National Happiness. He brought air travel and television to Bhutan, and tourism."

Ugyen waggled his head. "Yes," he said. "The king is a very good king."

As we drove, I noticed a number of fires on the mountainsides—mountains are everywhere, the entire nation within the Himalayan mountain range—and asked whether they were being used to clear the mountain for pasture, or if they were wildfires. They both looked at the hillside as if they hadn't noticed.

"No, they are just fires," Pema said.

"So will crews come to put them out?" It was rough terrain, and so not clear how a crew could even approach. "Or helicopters?"

"No, the rain will put them out." There wasn't a cloud in the sky.

"Is there a fire department?"

"No," Pema said.

"In city," Ugyen said.

"Yes, but we can't afford fire department over the whole country!" Pema said, smiling, like that should be obvious. All week, after that, I couldn't help seeing fires everywhere, waiting for rain.

Every tourist attraction in Bhutan is a religious site. The most famous, the Paro Taktsang Monastery, is the image you may have seen, the monastery clinging to the cliffside a mile up like a swallow's nest. It is a three- or four-hour hike up, slightly less if you ride a horse the first half, and slightly less on the way down. As Pema walked me up the mountain, he told the story of the tiger that had lived there and the saint who had welcomed the tiger into the monastery, part cave, part structure. We had been to a temple, a convent, a monastery, and a stupa the day before. In each one, Pema gave long disquisitions on the artwork—art that was always related to a part of scripture or myth or doctrine—and outlined the history of the place, which was always a religious history. He had a very close and personal relation, he implied, with all fourteen Dalai Lamas and an equal number of Panchen Lamas, and in temples with hundreds of statues, he liked to identify and say something about each and every one of them.

Both he and Ugyen have altars in their houses, where they make daily offerings, sometimes involving prostrations, always prayers, and they prayed while they were on the road too. Much of Pema's daily religious life seemed rote, habitual, hardly registering in his consciousness, and yet at times he would fall into a devotional moment and send the prayer wheel singing— there are many of every size in Bhutan, from teacup to gallon jar to oil drum to ten feet high and seven across. The big ones tended to catch his attention and induce an actual prayer.

I pestered him a little about his beliefs, wanting to know whether he was a fundamentalist, literalist, or if the stories of this buddha or that king or the monkey god were metaphors, archetypes—that is, ways to understand the world even if not the literal, historical truth. He considered the question for a while, eyes squinting, looking at the base of a tree past my feet.

"I think it is both," he said.

"Both true and not true?"

"Yes, both. I believe both things."

My last day, I asked them to take me to see the real city, the kind of place they went on their night off, no tourists, no religion, and Pema got excited.

"Yes!" he said. "I know what to do!"

Ugyen looked at him sideways, and Pema explained in Dzongkha, the language of Bhutan. Ugyen shook his head.

"Is this a bad idea?" I asked Ugyen. He did his noncommittal head waggle.

"You will see, you will love this!" Pema said, while Ugyen stayed uncomfortable. What would it be? I wondered. A dance club, maybe, something a little too risqué for Ugyen and too expensive for Pema on his own hook but made possible if I paid our way. That was the vibe I was getting from the little they weren't translating for me. Or, I thought, maybe Pema wanted to take me to some speakeasy, that it was just about drinking—the only time either of them had imbibed in the ten days we were together was at the home-cooked meal, where we were served some pretty weak homemade hooch— and watching them with that showed how infrequently they drank—Pema had gotten even more voluble and Ugyen even quieter. I hadn't seen a bar or liquor store.

After dinner they picked me up, for the first time wearing Western clothes rather than traditional dress. We walked a few blocks into what looked like a bar, although it was very dark, and hard to see. All the other patrons were men. The low-rent furniture—chairs, partial booths, rickety tables—was haphazard, scavenged, and scattered around. At the far side of the room, some weak colored lights drew a small stage out of the murk. A half dozen young women, in traditional dress—skirts to the floor, sleeves to the wrists, neckline all the way up, shapeless—milled around to the right. One of them came over and took our drink order. Sure enough, we were in some Bhutanese version of a gentleman's club. We ordered beers and sat, tried to talk, but the music— also traditional—was loud, lo-fi, and trebly. Five of the women took to the stage, two of them holding wireless mikes, a new song started, and they sang along. All five danced, a sedate, swaying, almost somnolent dance as they sang a song that, as Pema explained, was about the beauty and soul of Bhutan, a song that everyone knew well. Pema said he didn't know how old it was, maybe fifty years, maybe older. There wasn't the slightest hint of sexuality in any of their gestures or movements, but in every other way, this was like a strip club, the male gaze fixated. When the women weren't on stage, they circulated among the men and talked to them, although there was no touching, much less sitting on laps. Part of their job, as in a strip club, was to get the men to order drinks.

One young woman was assigned to me because she spoke English, and after some preliminaries, like where we were from, I asked what she thought the future might hold for her. She seemed confused by the question.

"I don't know," she said. "The future . . ."

"Well, what is your dream?" I asked, and she perked up.

"Princess Diana!" she said. "Oh, I love her so much! She is dead, and she has two children, her name was Diana Spencer—I know everything!" She went on for a while about Diana's life, how beautiful she was, how hard her life was. I asked if that was what she wanted, then, for the future, to be a British princess. She laughed and said, no, of course not. She wanted, she said, to be a professional singer and songwriter. She had written some songs already. Her best, in her opinion and people told her, was an ode to the beauty and soul of Bhutan.

The other young women continued to sing on the stage. Ugyen looked extremely uncomfortable, almost morose. I suggested to Pema that we leave since it was clear Ugyen was having a bad time, but Pema had a buzz on from his two beers and wasn't the least bit concerned about Ugyen or anyone else. I saw how young he was, still a fledgling man confused by sex, even in this most G-rated version.

And yet. Perhaps the strangest thing about Bhutan, given its general puritanism, is the iconography of the penis, which is everywhere. Dicks with hairy balls are painted on the sides of buildings, often in the process of ejaculating, a spray headed into the sky. These are not offhand graffiti but the work of penis artists, who construct large murals, small wall decorations, and everything in between. Other artisans carve tens of thousands of phalluses out of wood, some dildo-sized, some six feet tall. Everyone seems to be perfectly comfortable with these penises spurting all over town, especially in Chimi Lhakhang, the town where the fifteenth-century Tibetan saint Drukpa Kunley, also known as the Divine Madman, first taught Buddhism to the locals. The Divine Madman was a roving Tibetan teacher of Buddhism who was said to have decided where he was going to spread the word (and his own seed) next by shooting an arrow into the sky and preaching wherever it landed. One of the arrows he shot landed in Chimi Lakhang. The closest border with Tibet was more than fifty miles away, so he was a mighty archer, apparently. He spread not just the gospel of the Buddha but a lot of love too, taking lovers and wives and fathering children everywhere he went. The temple dedicated to him is where infertile couples go to get blessed and pregnant, and it is the epicenter of the represented penis. There and in town it adorns the walls of homes, restaurants, stupas, and walls. Shops have carved phalluses in the window, on shelves, hanging from the rafters. These are not pornographic images and objects but symbols of fertility, meant to be no more provocative than an image of a flower with its pistil, a peacock with its feathers spread, or a rearing stallion.

But although the ejaculating penis is everywhere, female skin, except on the hands or face, is nowhere to be seen. Not even in the gentlemen's clubs. The penises—comic, many of them, with single line hairs sparsely poking out of the ball sack like an adolescent's drawing, a fleur-de-lis of cum sprayed on the wall—are considered unremarkable, nonincendiary. But women draped from top of the neck to toe in traditional robes, singing traditional songs along with a karaoke machine, were so sexually provocative that boy-men leaned forward in their chairs, and poor Ugyen was so rattled he had to leave.

Closed off from the world for centuries, Bhutan opened its doors for the first time in 1974, when a total of 287 tourists came and saw a land and culture frozen in time. In the forty-five years since, the airport has been upgraded twice, and the infrastructure now supports a thousand times that many tourists. All guides and drivers and hotel clerks wear traditional dress, and the airport buildings are done in the style of the traditional wooden buildings. A combination of leftover traditions and tradition by policy and royal decree keep Bhutan Bhutanese. The archers in the parks — in Bhutan archery is the equivalent of golf in the US or bocce in Italy, something men of different ages do in groups — don't have to wear traditional dress, but they do, in the same way golfers customarily wear polo shirts. At the same time, the king, in his traditional dress, breaks with precedent by posing like a Sears model, relaxed, playing with his children on the floor, his wife with a salon hairdo but also playing with the children, all in a carefully managed presentation of themselves as everyday people, not divine beings. The kingdom, as the newspaper reports, plans on graduating from "least developed nation" status any day now. The largest newspaper is government owned, and the independent papers are famously self-censoring. As one journalist said, it is a small country, and you never know whose shoes you are stepping on. And a related sense of decorum pervades the society, from the temples to the shops to the parks full of archers.

The archery is astounding, by the way—the men shoot arrows at targets a hundred yards and more away, and as I watched the first time I thought it had to be impossible. A group of men, three or four, are set up on one side of the field, and three or four on the other, and they take turns, using what look like homemade bows and arrows, shooting long arcing shots the length of an entire football field and more at a three-feet-in-diameter bull's-eye-style target on an easel stand. Each archer gets three arrows a turn. The first shot I saw hit the dirt only a few feet short, which surprised me. The second went a little wide, making the far team move out of the way. And the third stuck deep into the target. It had a miraculous feel to it, like a goalie kicking a soccer ball from one end of the field straight through the air into the opposite goal. The level of skill, for the hour I sat there, was astronomical.

I was having trouble with the cord I used to download photos to my computer, so I went to a small shop that sold things phone or computer related. The owner had trouble matching it, so we had time to chat. When he heard I was a writer, he called his wife. She came from their house and brought a copy of her book of poetry. It was in English. It was self-published. It was not very good, as far as I could tell, but then again, it was my first Bhutanese poetry. Like the Princess Diana–loving songwriter in the bar, the wife of the guy at the electronics shop was creating art in that same vortex of tradition and modernity. The guy himself had crossed completely over. He was modern, wired, and everything in his store shouted globalization. He was a decent guy, liked heavy metal, and his wife had a beautiful earnestness. Her poetry was following some model that I assumed was from the Bhutanese past, rhyming and a bit singsong. I asked if she was following a specific form, but she thought she was just writing poetry, she said, she didn't think about it that way. Some of the poems about nature, she said on second thought, were like other poems of nature she had read.

I said the fact that she was writing in English suggested she was interested in the contemporary world as well as tradition, and she agreed she was interested in both. I asked them how they saw the monarchy, and the wife said she thought the royal family set a good example. I asked the husband if he agreed, as he sat among his busy displays of sim cards and phones and piles of electronic parts. Did he think that the king had found the right balance? He smiled and shrugged. He just didn't care. A kind of happiness, I suppose.

TAIWAN

The host of the radio show had some English, but not a lot; my friends Jeff and Eileen, who had arranged for me to be there and who were guests on the show as well, were fluent in Chinese; plus, the host had brought his boyfriend along to be a translator for me. The host was brash and loud and fun—he had a radio entertainer's ability to keep things at a high pitch of hilarity and intrigue— while the boyfriend was quiet and careful, almost shy. The boyfriend appreciated the host's audacity, sometimes with an intake of breath and a wry smile. He was also very polite, so when the conversation got rolling pretty fast in Chinese, he didn't like to interrupt, and large portions were never translated. I used my extralinguistic superpower and managed, through some fleeting proper nouns and reading body language, to keep up a little and even respond a little, to everyone's surprise. I've written about this before—opening all one's senses while listening to a conversation in a foreign language can allow for a fairly full emotional connection to the conversation, even with little shared vocabulary. People tell me I'm undoubtedly getting it wrong, which is true, but we get it wrong when we share a vocabulary too. I was in the mix.

The host was very smart, more AM zany than FM chill, and while this helped keep things moving, it made translation harder. We talked about many things. We were there for an important anniversary in Chinese history, which Jeff and Eileen covered—Jeff is a historian of China, Eileen was born in Taiwan and is also a scholar of Chinese and Taiwanese history and culture. Eventually, we came around to my travel writing. One thing the host couldn't get over was how a person could manage it all—it seemed an impossibility to him, an unthinkable extravagance to have traveled to as many places as I write about in my books. He and Eileen had an exchange about it, which is how I learned that the word "privilege" had been adopted by Taiwanese Chinese speakers and was now part of the vocabulary. I explained that I traveled cheaply—I ride buses and tuk-tuks, eat at street stands, and don't stay at tourist hotels but at cheap local places, where I rent rooms for as little as fifty cents or a dollar a night—so cheaply, in fact, that I spend less money on the road than I spend at home. He wasn't buying it.

"The time!" he said.

I explained that as a writer and editor, my office was my laptop, and that I actually got more work done on the road, not less, because I didn't have social obligations, didn't waste time watching TV, didn't have to take care of my house—I had more time for work on the road, not less.

"The flights!" he said. "Expensive!" I explained that I chose where to travel based on where routes were discounted, I went places off-season, that my flexibility meant that I could hop up and go when prices dropped precipitously, that I chose the days I flew based on price, that I took odd combinations of flights with multiple twelve-hour layovers that gave me forty-hour flights, which was fine because I just used that layover time to work in my laptop office—and that this all meant the flights weren't that prohibitive.

What Eileen had been telling him was that I recognized my privilege and talked about it in the books, that it was precisely that recognition that fueled some of what I wrote. This is true, but only partly so. It is impossible in poor countries not to feel the entitlement involved in having arrived there, when so few of them had the ability to visit the US, and not to feel it constantly, impossible not to understand the gross inequity my being there represents—I spend time with many people who live on less than one percent of my income. I often find it impossible not to recognize this in telling the story of being there, but not always, not everywhere.

And Taiwan, of course, is a special case. Whatever the pockets of rural poverty and pockets of urban poverty, it is a wealthy country. Its per capita GDP, corrected for PPP (parity purchasing power) places it between Saudi Arabia and Sweden, ranking sixteenth in the world (the US is eleventh). A sense of my own privilege was not the driving sense of my time there or of my relation to the radio host and his boyfriend. The night before, I had been at Ningxia night market, anchored by the historic octagonal Red House and surrounded by shopping and entertainment venues. A two-story-high picture of Lebron James dunking a basketball adorned one wall of the mall, and the square was full of the Taiwanese contingent of the international bourgeoisie, eating and shopping with friends and family, most of them wearing more expensive clothes than mine, none of us *that* much more or less privileged than the rest—all in the global top tenth. The high school kids had a lot of disposable income.

Elaine took me to a bookstore in downtown Taipei, the world's largest and the most impressive bookstore I've ever seen. Besides many floors of books, it had a museum-quality, multifloor exhibit on the history of publishing. She then took me to one of the world's largest and most impressive squares and to one of the world's most extravagant and impressive cultural forms, the Beijing opera, at a very extravagant and impressive opera house. All of this was made possible by a level of wealth above that of most countries on earth.

As in many places, the rest of the country is not as wealthy as the capital, and as I drove south, along the west coast, across the mountains and back up the east coast, I found many different microeconomies. I stopped at a gas station, a hundred miles south of Taipei, where a woman was selling zongzi, the triangular sticky rice dumplings steamed in bamboo leaves, tied with a piece of twine. The gas station looked like it had been built forty or fifty years ago, with some chipped paint, some missing putty on the windows, and some dirt in the corners. One zongzi was almost a full meal, and they were a fraction of a US dollar each. The woman, who also pumped the gas, had a batch staying warm in an ancient electric crockpot, and it was the single most delicious piece of food I'd had in the country. Sitting alone on a two-lane blacktop deep in the southern mountains, she had a clientele, I assumed, mainly of truck drivers. That she could make what she considered a reasonable profit at that price, and that she was charging what the traffic would bear, suggests that not everyone in the country can afford LeBron James–branded sneakers.

In a small town twenty miles in from the coast, I

stopped at the central square, alongside a pretty river, right after the sun had set, and a young duo, the boy playing a guitar, and the girl a keyboard with programmed rhythm parts, played pop songs, or maybe their own songs, for a crowd that consisted of me, a couple of old people—who might have been sitting there despite rather than because of the entertainment—and a handful of the performers' friends. Other people, walking home from work or heading to a shop or restaurant, slowed down more often than they stopped. The musical equipment—the kids had a late-model keyboard, nice amps and PA speakers—was expensive; their tip bucket, when I dropped some Taiwanese dollars in, almost empty. So again, a level of affluence was necessary; they were not going to pay off that equipment with their tips. Also, the kids were good—they knew how to play their instruments, how to program the synthesizer, how to work the electronics to enhance their voices—all signs of free time and prosperity as well. I asked one of their friends where I should eat, and they sent me to a new, highly designed hipster joint that was "Italian" in that it had pasta dishes and espresso and Peroni beer on tap. The noodle dishes were more Chinese than Italian and inexplicably all came with a basket of fries on the side. The bill was just a few dollars, which said to me that the affluence wasn't that widespread, that for a restaurant to stay in business, even on the high end in this small-town place, it couldn't charge very much for a meal. Real wealth was concentrated in the capital.

Sun Moon Lake, at the top of the Central Mountain Range that runs through the center of the island, exists in its own economic ecosystem too. It's an old-fashioned summer resort, a touch of the Poconos or the Catskills, paddleboats for rent and hotels here and there at water's edge. One, a "boatel," had a prow sticking into the lake in front. The entire place seemed plucked from the 1950s except for the way the young tourists dressed, which was straight-ahead 2010s; the townies were less fashionable. In the small town with the largest cluster of hotels, the usual food and sweets and souvenir shops lined the roads, and most of the people strolling were eating something on a stick. A few salesmen pitched their wares loudly, including a man who tried to convince everyone of the astounding virtues of almond milk, served warm. "Good for lungs!" he said to anyone who would listen and to many who wouldn't. I had a sausage on a stick and was reminded that to be a single man in a family-based tourist spot is a sad assignment. I spent the day writing on my low-end hotel's skinny deck while a woman and her son, the hotel's entire staff, went about their chores with the closed-off mien of people who deal with tourists day in and day out. They and the rest of the town were not getting rich on the city folks frolicking, but they weren't starving either. A couple of people told me that the big money goes to Macao or Hong Kong or Thailand, that high season now was what low season used to be. There were too many hotels, too many people making sausages on sticks, too many tchotchke shops for the traffic to bear.

In Hualien, near the airport, with jets screaming overhead every few minutes, the busy sidewalk stands served oyster omelets or scallion pancakes for next to nothing. Up the road, at Jiufen, the tiny cobbled streets were packed, and a scallion pancake cost five times as much. A well-preserved town from a hundred years ago, Jiufen is one of the few bits of living history in a country that was thoroughly transformed after 1949. Plastered against the hillside, the tiny picturesque lanes traverse up and down as in the towns of the Amalfi coast, and the center is just a nonstop parade of tourist services: restaurant, sweet shop, tchotchke shop, coffee shop, "art" gallery, restaurant, ice cream shop, food on a stick, cotton candy, souvenir T-shirts, glowsticks, more sweets, roasted nuts, more tchotchkes. . . . The majority of tourists were day-trippers from the capital, spending money more freely than the Sun Moon Lake crowd, and twenty times as numerous. The main drag was shoulder to shoulder to shoulder to shoulder for a half mile.

After our radio show, the host gave us a little tour of the radio station. VOH Radio, or Voice of Han Radio, was started by the Chinese Defense Department in 1942 and moved with the Kuomintang to Taiwan in 1949. The station had a room where all its awards were displayed. The main award, like a radio Emmy or Peabody, was an old-school trophy—a cast aluminum microphone on a wooden base. Our announcer had won one but never had it presented to him because he had taken an ill-timed cigarette break. His parents were in the audience to see him get the award, and they watched as his name was called a few times before the show went on to the next award. For its first few decades, VOH Radio continued to aim anti-Communist broadcasts at the mainland. Starting in the 1980s, it diversified its programming and became a contemporary news and entertainment station. The sharp divide between the Communists and Nationalists, the People's Republic of China (PRC)

and the Republic of China (ROC), is commemorated in the glass cases and photographs of the little one-room radio museum, where the Nationalists are shown in their first years of exile and resistance. Standing in front of photographs of the earliest broadcasters, who had been chased out of China in 1949 by Mao and the Communists, I was reminded that this was a nation created by civil war, a conflict that has never been settled, that still hangs over everyday life, still requires diplomatic pas de deux and legerdemain, and which still leaves Taiwanese living in fear that they are the next Hong Kong, about to be forcibly reabsorbed by its insatiable other self.

When they arrived, the mainland Chinese found new conflict too, with the Taiwanese who had been there for centuries and who were, themselves, still in the process of trying to make amends to the Aboriginal tribes they had displaced. Perhaps the kindness I am proffered by strangers is the knowledge that I do not have a dog in any of their fights. I do not know the game, and I do not know the players. It makes a difference traveling through Oklahoma if you know the Trail of Tears, if you know who Andrew Jackson and Chief John Ross were, and even more if you know the Kiowa, Apache, Ute, and Comanche who lived there before the many other displaced tribes were pushed in. And although I can guess that the Taiwanese—I mean I don't have to guess, I can read—that the Taiwanese Aborigines were forced out of their lands by the Han from the mainland, that the history of Taiwan is now the result of the Han settlers in the same way that the history of America is the result of the European settlers, I don't have a lifetime of assimilating the stories. And without the stories, without knowing the attachments to place, without knowing the difference between the Cherokee in Georgia and the exiled Cherokee in Oklahoma, without knowing Taiwan's thirteen recognized Aboriginal peoples, without knowing their myths and lifeways, I know, and they know, that I cannot feel the facts of their history. Just as the Native nations of America have made people sit up and recognize their history in recent decades, so have the Aboriginal tribes of Taiwan started to reassert their culture and claims.

In practice, for the ignorant American like myself roving through the mountains, what this means is coming upon an Aboriginal village, an Aboriginal park, upon a fully touristic experience, informative, educational, cleaned up for a family-friendly presentation of song and dance and costume and glass-cased exhibits. But for anyone who has traveled in the Chinese hinterlands— in Xinjiang, in Tibet—it is easy to recognize the intense modernity and massive resettlement, the overwhelming power of Han settlement, trailing in its wake, as all settler colonialism does, a raft of injustices.

But as my host and my translator—the two of them so warm and considerate and openhearted—said goodbye to me and my friends outside the radio station, I thought about none of that—just about how, once again, perfect strangers had engaged with me, had taken the time to introduce themselves and their world, and had spent some time asking me about mine. Yes, it was the host's job to interview us, but he didn't have to give us a tour of the station, didn't have to bring his boyfriend in to translate for me, didn't have to extend himself the way he did: this was not a sense of duty, this was just the milk of human kindness. It is everywhere.

LA RÉUNION

A strange name for a strange place.

And yet somehow appropriate. The mix of races, the collapse of time and history—the past and present, the colonial and postcolonial, the European and African, the African and Indian, the Christian and Muslim and Hindu—a reunion of the global migration of the last hundred and more years. . . .

Four hundred miles east of Madagascar in the Indian Ocean, and a hundred miles southwest of Mauritius, it was uninhabited until settlers from France and Madagascar arrived in the seventeenth century, and so from the start it had a mixed population of immigrants. In my seafood restaurant run by a Parisian, two couples sat at small tables, all four of them mixed-race people, each of whom could have had ancestors on at least two continents; a third table had three coworkers, similarly mixed, and although at first glance I thought one was a white woman, she wasn't.

Which isn't to say there aren't white people—there are. This is France, after all, an overseas *département*, and the white people I met, like the restaurant owner and chef, were all French, some in Réunion for many generations. These French—ethnically French, everyone was technically French unless they were new immigrants— fell, it looked to me, into three distinct categories. Some were recent transplants, like the chef, but these were few. There were some classic colonial administrative and business class types—women in their seventies, for instance, in clothing modeled on Queen Elizabeth's, pastel and dark blue skirt-suits and pearls, beauty-shop updos and dowdy hats; a few older men in antique suits and ties, without the slightest glimmer of a nod toward their actual location in the world or their moment in history. And then the third group, guys who looked like they had spent their lives tooling around the Indian Ocean on rust buckets, getting in fights in a dozen minor ports, falling off their freighters drunk some night twenty years ago, just barely surviving since. Some might originally have been from France, some from Réunion, some undoubtedly from elsewhere. They had sun-damaged faces and long gray hair, not like hippies, but like guys who had given themselves their own last haircut and done it with a dull whaling knife a decade ago.

I asked a man in a camera shop, also white, about the racial makeup of the island, and he told me the law prohibits asking about race and ethnicity on official documents, including the census, so there are no reliable figures. He estimated that just shy of a quarter of the population is white, around a quarter Indian, and half Afro-Malagasy or, like the group in my restaurant, mixed.

On the average street in Saint-Denis, though, where 135,000 of the island's million people live, mixed-race people were the rule, and Indians outnumbered whites—whites, if I had to guess, were much scarcer than the man supposed. The few very white, very unassimilated people I saw reminded me of whites in South Africa, where such unreconstructed representatives of the colonial past also walk the streets bemoaning their lost power. Ghosts, they seemed. It wasn't only the skin color but the pearls and the pointedly out-of-date style. They weren't just white, and they weren't just French, they were early twentieth-century French, end-of-empire French. They didn't all share the same attitude—the lunching ladies were imperious and stridently conservative, the long-haired men dissolute and a bit Bohemian—as if the women were descended from the governors and the men from pirates. But they all had the air of people who had somehow been misplaced.

This is unfair, of course, more a projection of mine than anything else; and many of the French people I talked to, like the owner of the seafood restaurant, who had a Parisian self-confidence and self-possession, clearly felt not at all displaced but contentedly at home in their world.

The next night, after I'd been walking for miles, I got back to find the gated courtyard of my apartment building bustling, twenty or more people talking a mile a minute, going through plastic cases full of equipment and suitcases full of clothes and gear, scuba tanks and large plastic cases and backpacks, in the small courtyard. At first I thought they were a film crew. They were French—European French, not African French—and told me they were all part of an oceanographic research team. There were forty or more of them altogether, most scientists, but a few sailors and logistics people. They were doing a full survey of all the African islands in the Indian Ocean except Madagascar—another team was doing that big island in the middle of them all. Dozens and dozens of islands, many tiny and some uninhabited, some of which I knew, like Mauritius and the Comoros and Mayotte archipelagos, but most of which I had no idea existed—the Chagos, Tromelin, Bazaruto, and Quirimbas archipelagos, the Glorioso Islands, Rodriguez, the Agaléga Islands—all spread a thousand miles north and south and a thousand miles east and west. The national status of some of these dots in the ocean is contested, and the French drop a pair of soldiers on a number of them to "hold" them against invaders; the total population of some of them is just those two soldiers.

The oceanographers said the soldiers are happy to see them because otherwise they can go months without a visitor. Some of these researchers knew the ropes and had taken similar trips, but several were going for the first time, and there was a certain amount of nervousness and anxiety as well as excitement in the group. Some of them would be dropped by the ship at one of the contested islands to live with the two soldiers for a month or two while they made all their measurements and observations and readings, with no chance of leaving, no redress, no company, and no commerce in all that time, until the boat returned to pick up them and their data.

It made me think of *Robinson Crusoe* and the Japanese soldiers holding Pacific islands for the emperor, decades after the war ended, nobody to tell them the news.

"Don't you get lonely out there, on an island by yourself for months?"

"You know," he said, "if you love your research"—it sounded like *recherche*—"it is quite exciting to be in the collecting stage. You feel in communication with other scientists, you are talking to them in your notes, in your discoveries." He thought for a minute. "Sometimes the soldiers are good company." And then, "But yes, sometimes."

His friend added: "It's nice to be appreciated. The soldiers like to see me, and I like to see them each morning. In Paris, maybe we are not friends, but in the Indian Ocean," he said with a laugh, "it is a beautiful relationship."

I arrived, my first day, in the evening, and by the time I had rented a car and got the keys to my room from the very helpful Paulette—she lived in one of the other apartments and managed the place—it was already dark. The building was perched on the edge of Saint-Denis, in a neighborhood without much commercial activity, and fresh from the airport, I hadn't stopped to pick up any water or supplies. A pizza place across the street had already closed, and the only activity was around a mosque a half block away. I walked over to a young man with a beard, skullcap, and long white kaffiyeh, who had just parked his car. His wife and son walked toward the mosque as he locked the doors and grabbed a book from the dash. I asked in French whether he knew if there was a store nearby, and he shook his head sadly, thought a minute, and said no, the closest was about a mile and, *c'est dommage,* probably—he glanced at his watch—closed already as well. He asked what I needed, and I said I just wanted to buy some water. Oh! he said and unlocked his car, popped open the hatchback and rummaged a minute, pulling out an enormous bottle of water—five liters—and offered it to me.

"Oh, no!" I said. "Thank you so much, but that is too much, I couldn't!" and then realized I was speaking English. *"Ce n'est pas possible!"*

"Oui, oui, pas de problem, ceci c'est ma plaisir," he said.

It was clear from his car—far from new, a little banged

up, small for a family—that he was not a rich man. Flustered, my French got progressively worse, but it didn't matter. We both knew the situation we were in. I protested, he insisted, I tried to offer some money for it, he refused, and pushed the water into my hands. I expressed my deep gratitude as best I could, told him he was *muy gentile*, mixing my French with Spanish, and in the end, our eyes met for a last time, and I acknowledged his thoughtfulness, again, as best I could, and he let me see he appreciated the attempt.

Perhaps, in a world where Muslims get so much bad press, there was an incentive for him to reach out with a counterpresence, but perhaps he was just a kind and generous person. At any rate, I didn't want to keep him from joining his family any longer, so I didn't hold him up and ask any more questions, just thanked him again and bowed. I thought perhaps he was in an intellectual trade of some sort—he had a scholarly air about him, and he had stopped to grab a book—but maybe not, maybe he was just people smart, and he was grabbing a prayer book. In any case, I felt that even if he had multiple motivations, foremost among them was what seemed not like an exception but like a habit of reflexive helpfulness. It wasn't much really—just a big jug of water—but I walked away once again astounded at the abundance of human kindness in this world.

The representatives of the human race I keep bumping into around the globe have been, like this young family man on his way to prayers, more than anything else, naturally and spontaneously compassionate and welcoming. This shouldn't be surprising: we're social animals, and we require networks just to survive, much less to build airlines and publishing houses and radio stations and databases of oceanographic surveys. By nature we cooperate, and when we stop doing so, it is often because we feel threatened, we feel we have been wronged, we feel we deserve justice and are not getting it.

Back in my room, I couldn't stop thinking about the extraordinary amount of kindness that is exhibited by people every day, in tiny ways and larger ones, and more often than not these kindnesses are offered to total strangers, just as we sometimes offer them to total strangers at home. We have, in the US, become newly attuned to how microaggressions work, how they enforce our differences, but while I'm sure it makes me seem like some doe-eyed sentimentalist, I think it is worth recognizing the microkindnesses we do each other every day, as well. A bottle of water. The gift of a simple conversation about researching the islands of the Indian Ocean, scattered up and down the east coast of Africa. A tour of a Taiwanese radio station.

At home, I take these gifts for granted; I think of them as normal, as people just following the norms of their culture, but so often, on the road, there is no norm, or at least I have no idea what the norms are. I am not supposed to be there. I have no place in the culture, I have no meaning as anything but a stranger. And yet everywhere I go I am met with benevolence, with hospitality, with interest. This man on the way to the mosque. The women in my lunchroom in Tajikistan, my guides and their friends in Madagascar and Mongolia, the wedding parties in Uzbekistan and Ethiopia, the strangers who let me into their lives for a moment in the Philippines, Nepal, Brazil, Bangladesh, and Bhutan. What a wonderful species we are when we're not killing each other.

What wonderful people. What kindness. What a wonderful world.

ACKNOWLEDGMENTS

Thanks to, over there—Ariel Saramandi, Togos Togosoo, Joël Raijo, Sabed Hossain, Myriam López, Nadeem Zaman, Suzanne Wiradimedjo, Samrawit Mussie, Moges Wedaje, Mustafo Tolibov, Sosina Haileselassie, and the many other kind people I met on these travels; here *and* there Elias Wondimu, Eileen Chow, and Jeff Wasserstrom; in the book biz—BJ Robbins, Boris Dralyuk, Irene Yoon, Jim McCoy, Carolyn Brown, Jacob Roosa, Karen Copp, Susan Hill Newton, and Allison Means; and here at home, my colleagues and students at UC Riverside, Paul Mandelbaum, Seth Greeland, master debriefer Jon Wiener, partner in crime Albert Litewka, and as always, Laurie Winer: first reader, best reader.